Gone Native

called by the curlew and the beat of drums

Donald MacIntosh

MERLIN UNWIN BOOKS

Published by:
Merlin Unwin Books Ltd
Palmers House
7 Corve Street
Ludlow
Shropshire SY8 1DB
U.K.

www.merlinunwin.co.uk

The author asserts his moral right to be identified with this work.

Designed and set in Minion Pro by Merlin Unwin
Printed in Great Britain by the MPG Books Group

ISBN 978 1 906122 26 3

CONTENTS

We shall not cease from exploration
And the end of all our exploring
Will be to arrive where we started
And know the place for the first time

T. S. Eliot *Four Quartets*
Little Gidding V

CHAPTER ONE

God Smoked a Clay Pipe

Can you recall, dear comrade, when we tramped God's land together,
And we sang the old, old Earth-song, for our youth was very sweet;
When we drank and fought and lusted, as we mocked at tie and tether,
Along the road to Anywhere, the wide world at our feet.

Robert W. Service *The Tramps*

To most of those inhabiting my small world back then, I don't suppose he was worth a brass farthing. To them, he was only my grandfather. But to me, he was God.

Mind you, even I would have to admit that he didn't look much like the Calvinistic idea of God, now that I allow my mind to drift back to those childhood years from the comfort zone of my allotted three score years and ten and a bit. But I had no identification crisis with him, for he was my God, and far superior to any other God, Calvinistic or otherwise, that anyone ever tried to foist upon me, then or in later life. I have been without him for three score of these years now, but my memory of him is as clear as though he were still with me. One doesn't forget one's God as easily as that, not when one has known him as intimately as I did.

He was not, by any means, a big man. He might have stood about seventeen hands high in his hobnailed boots if the wind was not too strong, but he couldn't have weighed much more than a sack of newly dug potatoes, soaking wet. His shoulders were permanently bowed, like the shoulders of the stunted scrub oak along the western shores of his beloved Isle of Mull. Like the oaks, he seemed to be forever stooping away from fierce Atlantic gales. His face was the colour of last year's bracken at the end of a hard winter, and the southern shores of his raggedy grey moustache were stained the colour of Highland toffee, like a fringe of muddy lace hanging from an unwashed crinoline petticoat.

One didn't need the olfactory powers of a nocturnal predator to know when my grandfather was about: the clean freshness that one rapidly comes to associate with the bracing air of Galloway would be instantly replaced with a powerful miasma of heavy-duty tobacco smoke and that curious Old Man Smell by which you could identify the true countryman back in those days before effeminate cologne manufacturers poisoned women's minds and encouraged them to ensure that their poor men smelled less like men and more like Armenian eunuchs. There would be times when this atmospheric ripeness would be further enriched by a fragrance emanating from a bottle of amber fluid which he kept hidden for emergencies behind the bed in his little room. This, he once told me, contained an elixir named 'Distillery Potion', the only known prophylactic against an ailment named 'acute melancholia', prevalent among elderly Hebrideans in times of stress, such as when my mother was embarking upon the annual saturnalia known as spring-cleaning. At such times the Distillery Potion would come into its own. The bottle would be secreted in a haversack along with a few comestibles for my consumption and we would head off over the fields for the sanctuary of Crow Wood, plumes of smoke erupting defiantly from him like a Clyde puffer chugging up the North Minch in the teeth of a strong nor'wester.

For all of the decade in which he was to be everything that mattered in life to me, his sole ensemble would consist of a pair of moleskin trousers, a jacket and waistcoat of the coarsest black serge, a collarless blue-striped shirt that might once upon a time have been white, and a bunnet of a curious sort of loden hue unknown in the annals of art or nature. Hobnailed boots liberally coated with dubbin completed a mode of vesture that stamped him forever as being more of the people than of the *beau monde*. I never knew him to be dressed in any other way, even on the rare occasions on which he could be persuaded to trundle down the road with us of a Sunday to the wee kirk beyond the burn.

Other worshippers tended to give us a wide berth; after all, they had their best holy clothes on, and it is doubtful whether they regarded the old man as being enough of a fashion state-ment at the best of times to be worthy of their presence. My mother would make the occasional barbed comment about her mortification at having to be seen on the Sabbath Day in the presence of a damned old tinker, but I do not remember giving too much thought to the matter back then except to opine to myself that he was, after all, God, and was thus surely entitled to dress however the hell he liked.

Mind you, he was always enough of a gentleman to remove his bunnet and extinguish his pipe before entering the kirk to pay his respects to this alien God of the Scottish Lowlands, and I do not ever recall him spitting during the sermons, a feat of remarkable restraint since country-church sermons in those days were not only singularly protracted and of excruciating boredom, but in Galloway, were conducted in English, a language of which my Gaelic grandfather knew only a few vital swear words.

I suppose the old man's *pièce de résistance* had to be his clay pipe. Seldom, if ever, can a more disgraceful object have been found stuck in the mouth of a civilised man.

Clay pipes are virtually unheard of nowadays, but in my youth they were all the rage among the proletariat. Short of stem and made of a white kaolinic clay, their popularity owed much to the fact that they cost no more than a penny. My grandfather's pipe cost him nothing. He found it in a barrow of cow manure while he was planting potatoes. A piece of binder twine pulled vigorously through the stem and a cursory rinsing at the pump did not, admittedly, remove all traces of its lengthy immersion in the manure, but it was good enough for the old man.

He knew that the viscous green dung stain would soon vanish under the evil cankerous coating produced by the Bogie Roll plug tobacco he smoked; a brand of tobacco, incidentally, without which no real clay pipe aficionado could possibly feel truly fulfilled. Treacly black nicotine gurgled merrily in the shank and oozed down the sides of the bowl as he sucked contentedly, and he was an expert with the sneaky shot across the bows from the cargo of sputum produced therefrom. I once saw him frighten the life out of a passing sparrow at a range of at least seven paces with a jet of the noxious fluid, fired from its launching pad in the region of his tonsils at something approaching the speed of light.

I have never smoked in my life, nor have I ever felt tempted to do so: with a class act like the old man to follow, I should have always been dogged by an inferiority complex when it came to the spitting part of the exercise.

There was a certain feyness about him, as there is, I think, with many Hebrideans. It was a feyness that manifested itself in a decided gloominess of demeanour, a Highland gloom that seemed to lift only when he was alone with me. For the first ten years of my life and the last ten years of his, he lived with us in Galloway, southern Scotland, far from his native Isle of Mull. He might as well have been in Outer Mongolia. He did not speak English, and the Gallovidians did not speak his language. Gallovidians are the friendliest of people, and I am certain that, had he made the slightest effort, he would have been less of the lonely character that he obviously was. But he made no effort. Perhaps the language barrier was too great. Perhaps – much more likely – he had no interest in making friends with strangers in a strange land. Perhaps he was content with what he had: a grandson with whom he could converse freely in his native tongue, to whom he could tell Hebridean fairy tales in our secret enclave among the bracken of our enchanted Crow Wood; someone who worshipped him as no one had ever done before or ever would again.

The Crow Wood was our private retreat, our personal Shangri-la. It was to the Crow Wood that we repaired when we wanted to escape from the tribulations of life. There were times when I went there on my own and occasions when I was accompanied by my siblings. But the times I liked best were when the old man and I went to the wood together, just the two of us.

In a way, the Crow Wood was a bit like the old man in that it was not much to look at, on first sight. You had to catch it on a good day to see it at its best. It consisted of a strip of unkempt woodland half a mile to the south of our cottage, flanked by a pretty little brook full of trout on its western side. It got its name from the rookery that occupied its southern half, the tall, slender, whippy elms there making ideal nesting sites for the hundreds of rooks that came in from the surrounding fields. Early springtime was nesting time for them, and we avoided this section of the wood then, for not only was their clamour raucous and deafening, but the steady drizzle of ordure from the high tops would have repelled all but the most dedicated of ornithologists. The greenish-grey slime was almost impossible to remove from clothing, and it stank to high heaven. At nesting time, we contented ourselves with watching the antics of the birds from the edge of the rookery. They quarrelled constantly and with ferocity, and they exhibited all the less attractive characteristics of the human race. They took transparent delight in stealing from their neighbours, often for no obvious reason, filching sticks from nests when the occupants were absent.

They were terrible racists, too. A strange rook with a few white feathers in its tail appeared from nowhere one day as we were watching. It was instantly mobbed and harried by the others, two of its white feathers being plucked unceremoniously from its bottom as it fled.

The Crow Wood was at its best in the springtime. In winter, even when it was not raining, you would get soaked. The tree branches and the dead bracken dripped with cold water and even the rooks were silent. At this time of the year the wood was as bleak and miserable as anything to be found in the fairy tales of the brothers Grimm. In summer, countless legions of the dreaded Scottish midges roosted in the green bracken, the slightest touch against a stem sending a ripple like a Mexican Wave through the fronds and arousing clouds of the voracious insects into a veritable feeding frenzy for which there was only one repellent – the fumes from the old man's pipe.

Autumn was the time of gales. The Irish Sea was only a few miles over to the west and the wind would come screaming in from the Cruggleton Rocks and over the flat fields, thrashing the slender elms branches to a fury against each other and sending cascades of dead sticks and other debris tumbling from the old nests to the ground far below.

But springtime in the Crow Wood – ah then, how different *that* was! In springtime, the Crow Wood was a paradise of colour and birdsong and magic, and it was a joy to be alive. The wind had lost its bite and it was not yet warm enough to bring the midges out from their winter lodgings. The curly green heads of the bracken were just beginning to push their way through the bronze of last year's growth, while in her secret refuge under the shelf of the burn the shy primrose was beginning to show her pretty little head in a rapture of gold. Vines of forget-me-not trailing along the burn bank were already a faint haze of Wedgwood blue, while, in the small damp hollow in the centre of the wood, the brazen marsh marigold sported her gold-plate headdress, like a harlot setting off for a night on the town.

On a dry little hillock at the edge of the wood, the royal-blue of the fragile violet vied for attention with the equally delicate bugle and heartsease. The scent of so many varieties of flowers was heady and somehow feminine in its fragrance when one was resting on the ground, but the moment one stood up, the trees took over: the aphrodisiac cedar-scent of the Douglas Fir, the turpentine aroma of the Scots Pine and Silver Fir, the fruity orange-smell of the solitary Giant Fir that stood like a sentinel at the entrance to the wood, and many more.

This was a time of the year when birds were competing with each other in song, and the section of the wood not occupied by the rooks was a veritable orchestra of avian music. The happy carolling of the chaffinch rang ceaselessly through the high tops and the piping call of the pink-breasted bullfinch could be heard from the soft-hued larch fronds at the far corner of the wood. Wrens and warblers trilled their roundelays from thickets of elderberry and briar, and the soft – yet oddly penetrating – zee-zee-zee of the tiny goldcrest, Britain's smallest bird, could be heard from the majestic Scots Pine. High overhead, somewhere up there where cotton-wool tufts of cloud drifted lazily over an azure sky, the unforgettable melody of the skylark paid endless tribute to the deity who made this perfection possible.

Looking back on it all now it seems that most of the really important parts of my childhood were spent in the Crow Wood with my grandfather. School interrupted my fun to a certain extent when I reached the age of five years and had to walk daily down to the village to get a more formal education, but even so, there was always time after school to toddle up to the Crow Wood with the old man. He had had very little schooling himself, but he was the best teacher I ever had. Listening to him under the chestnut tree in the Crow Wood, I learned all I ever needed to know about survival on this earth, and I learned a lot about the old man's unique philosophy on life after our time on this earth was over.

The chestnut tree was big and old, with a huge spreading crown that gave shade from the glare of the sun and gave shelter when it rained. From the beginning the old man had adopted it as a base for our explorations and talks. It was conveniently sited, too, being just on the fringe of the section inhabited by the rooks. There, we could sit and watch their activities in comfort without being constantly splattered upon. With our backs to the great bole, I would listen avidly while he told me fables he had learned in childhood, tales about Gaelic demigods like Duncan of the Long Axe and Deirdre of the Sorrows.

There was a cavity in the bole of the tree and in this recess he kept an oilskin pouch containing a spare clay pipe and a roll of tobacco. It was 'in case of emergency', he said. I never found out what kind of emergency he envisaged for I never saw him dip into the contents. I think it was just his insurance against the event of a disaster, such as breaking the stem of his 'good' pipe or my mother confiscating his tobacco.

It was under the chestnut tree, too, that he found a new interest in life and it was one with which, to my intense delight, I was able to help. At the end of my first year in school, *The Dandy* comic first saw the light of day. The old man took an instant liking to it. He could not, of course, read the English script so I had to translate as best as I could. Desperate Dan was an immediate favourite with him. 'A fine, strapping fellow,' was his verdict. 'He must have been a Mull man. I'm surprised he didn't have the Gaelic.'

The old man was an expert on the tin whistle. He had got the whistle many years before, he said, from a tinker in Mull in exchange for a rubbery old coalfish that no one else would look at. On days so drab as to put a temporary halt to our explorations he would produce the whistle and the sad melodies of the Hebrides seemed to hang in the still, wet air. When he played the movingly poignant air *An t'Eilean Muileach* (The Isle of Mull), it seemed as though every bird in the wood fell silent until the last silvery note had trilled out through the trees. I have heard it played many times by professional musicians, but never as hauntingly as when played in the Crow Wood by the old man on his cheap tin whistle. He even composed a tune especially for me, a tune which he called *Larks in the Dawning*.

This was the fey part of him coming to the surface: he always maintained that I was born a wanderer and would thus sleep in the open with the larks in many countries throughout my life.

He was a superstitious as a spae-wife. The carrion crow, he said, was a cousin of Satan, and the sight of one roosting in a tree outside one's house was a sure sign that a member of the household was about to die. Also portenders of death were magpies, lapwings and ravens. Rooks, on the other hand were good birds and friends of humans. Indeed, he said, when a Hebridean died, the rook was the bird entrusted to carry his soul to Tir nan Og, the Gaelic Heaven.

'Where is Tir nan Og? Will there be a Crow Wood there? Are women allowed in there?' The questions came tumbling out of me.

The location of Tir nan Og depended upon which part of the Hebrides you came from, he said. Skye people went to the Isle of Raasay when they died, which served them jolly well right. Harris people spent eternity weaving hats for English grouse-shooters. Those with Muileach blood like ourselves, he said, would find the real Tir nan Og at the foot of Ben More on the Isle of Mull.

'Where will Jimmy Wilson the shepherd go?' I interrupted.

'Good God! Jimmy Wilson?' he cried with considerable feeling. 'That bugger borrowed my new sharpening stone to sharpen his bloody scythe last week and he broke the thing. He will go straight to hell, mark my words. Anyway, he's from Glasgow so he won't know the difference, poor ignorant creature that he is.'

'Tir nan Og,' he continued, 'is where all good people with Hebridean blood in their veins go when they die. One day, you will qualify, if your blood has not been too contaminated by your anglification at Garlieston Primary School, what with learning to speak English and singing *God Save Our Gracious King* and foreign rubbish like that. In Tir nan Og, he said, *The Dandy* comic will be written in Gaelic and Desperate Dan will be running a distillery. But women are certainly allowed into Tir nan Og, for they act as a civilising influence wherever they are. Man would descend to the gutter without women around him. They stop us spitting and drinking and swearing in the house, and they stop us making disgusting noises while we are having our porridge. Besides, they are prettier than men. They are good to have around for decorative purposes, if for nothing else.'

His pipe was empty. He took a strip of tobacco from the pouch and began to shave pieces with his penknife. The black fluid oozed like treacle between his fingers as he worked the tobacco to a pulp in the palm of his hand.

'That is,' he continued, 'if you can stop in one place long enough in your travels to appreciate them.'

I said something or other to him, but he wasn't listening. He was gazing outward, towards the northwest, towards the horizon, his mind and his eyes searching through the infinity of time and space towards his beloved Isle of Mull, to his Tir nan Og. He laid the pipe down at the foot of the tree and fumbled in his pocket for his tin whistle.

He left us suddenly and without fuss, as I should have expected. I remember that morning as though it were yesterday. I was on the way to school and as usual, he had walked with me down the rough track to the main road. He was, I remember, a little distant and quiet that morning, just smiling to himself as I chattered the foolish nonsense that children babble when they are sublimely happy, but I do not recall noticing anything unusual in his manner as we walked What was unusual was that, when we reached the road junction, he bent down before me and put his hands on my shoulders, his pale-blue, watery old eyes peering straight into mine. I thought that strange because he was the archetypal West Highlander in that he had never been a demonstrative person. There was a look in his eyes now, too, that I had never seen before, a withdrawn look, a wistful, indescribable look. His moustache looked even more moth-eaten than ever. It smelt strongly of tobacco and the ochrous colour of his teeth seemed even more pronounced as he smiled a strange, sad little smile at me.

'You'll soon me a man,' he whispered 'taking care of yourself. Make sure you do a good job of it. I've taught you all I can, and now it's up to you. I'm tired now, and it's time I had a good, long rest.'

I did not understand what he was trying to tell me. For the first time in my life, I was in the presence of Death, but I was too young to realise it. I tried to speak, but there was a hard, painful lump in my throat that I had never experienced before. I swallowed once, twice, but it wouldn't go away.

'Just do your best, wherever you are, whatever you're trying to do,' he continued, 'and you can't go far wrong.'

He straightened abruptly and smiled down at me.

'Better get off down that road to school,' he said, 'or you'll be late and we wouldn't want that, would we?'

He lit his pipe, puffing furiously, the blue smoke wreathing his head in an acrid cloud. I was turning to go when he said: 'Don't worry, my wee laddie. There'll be a Crow Wood in Tir nan Og when you come to see me. And you won't have to sing *God Save the King* there, either.'

He gave a throaty chuckle and turned away from me, walking back up the farm track in his loose-limbed, bow-shouldered way, a trail of tobacco smoke following him. I ran off down the road towards the village, running blindly, unseeingly, not once looking back, not daring to look back.

I knew for sure the moment I got home from school. It wasn't because Miss Hannay, the rather terrifying old spinster who owned the farm, was in our cottage, talking quietly to my mother, nor was it the sight of my mother's tense face. It was not even the fact that the curtains were drawn over the old man's bedroom window. I had, without knowing why, known all day that he wouldn't be around to greet me when I got home.

I put my schoolbag quietly into my room and slipped out of the house...

A drizzly rain had begun to fall but I was protected from the worst of it by the heavy curtain of leaves that crowned the chestnut tree. I sat there, my back resting against the tree, my mind numbed with shock, my head crowded with memories of the old man, thinking about him sitting here beside me, puffing away at his clay pipe, remembering the fluid notes of his tin whistle and the sweetness of the Hebridean melodies he produced from it, hearing again his gravelly voice as he told me yet another of his Gaelic stories.

A rook suddenly appeared out of the murk to alight on the topmost branch above me. It moved up and down the branch, sideways, restlessly, until it found a spot on the branch where it felt comfortable. It lifted one foot and picked at its claws solemnly with its long, coarse beak. Suddenly, it seemed to become aware of my presence. It peered down at me, neck outstretched and shoulders hunched, for all the world like the old man when he was about to deliver one of his homilies to me. It cawed twice, thrice, four times, its bright eye inquisitorial. It stretched its wing and gave it a cursory preening. It cocked its head to one side and peered down at me again. Then it gave one last caw and launched itself into the leaden sky. It wheeled once, slowly, around the Crow Wood, circling it one last time, then it veered sharply away over the farmlands, flying northwest with swift-beating wings, heading straight northwest as surely as though following a compass bearing, heading, as I knew it would, for Tir nan Og. I was waving when it was but a tiny dot in the distance, and I was still waving when there was nothing to wave at any more but the heavy grey clouds and the rain and the sodden trees around me.

A cold runnel of water trickled down my neck. I knew it was time to go. I turned up the collar of my jacket, then I remembered the old man's secret cache. I thrust my hand in. The oilskin package was still there. I took it out, opened it, looked at the clay pipe and the roll of tobacco, wondering whether to bury the lot behind the tree or take it home with me. I put it back in the recess and then, for no particular reason, stuffed a clump of bracken into the hole to camouflage it. He'll come back for it when he needs it, I reflected. And, I thought, I'll bring his bottle of Distillery Potion and his tin whistle with me tomorrow and put them in here with his pipe and tobacco. He's going to need his medicine and a wee tune to cheer him up when they start the spring-cleaning in Tir nan Og.

As I trudged homewards the heavens tipped their contents down upon me, relentlessly, drearily. A pair of curlews stooped and curvetted overhead, their plaintive cries echoing out over the stark fields. It was a fitting coronach to the end of childhood.

I was eleven years and one month old. Already, I had taken my first steps on the Road to Anywhere.

CHAPTER TWO

The Rattling Bog

'Blows the wind today, and the sun and the rain are flying,
Blows the wind on the moors today and now,
Where about the graves of the martyrs the whaups are crying,
My heart remembers how!'

Robert Louis Stevenson

They were a familiar sight in the autumnal gloamings of
my youth as my brother and I wended our way homeward
along the Old Bog Road. From all the airts they came surging
in, feathered armadas of them filling the sky with their swirling,
black confusion of traffic, endless masses of birds, soaring
and circling above and around that small splash of water far
below them, their whistling and chirruping and chattering
and whirring of wings sending the resident colony of whaups
lumbering into the air in a tumult of anxious funereal piping
calls. Round and round the invaders wheeled, column upon
column of them, looping the loop, performing figures of eight

victory rolls, Immelan turns, the sound of their passage like a faint roll of thunder in the distant Galloway hills. We never could figure out what all this complicated aerial manoeuvring was about, since the incomers always knew which tree or bush was theirs by right of conquest, each species of bird settling with their own fellows into the exact same tree or shrub or clump of reeds as they had done the previous evening and, most probably, every other evening before that since time immemorial, the starlings occupying the tall, solitary alder tree out in the middle of the water and the smaller birds such as the reed buntings and wagtails choosing the thin strands of crack-willow and bulrushes around the fringes of the lochan.

The bog was a noisy place to be anywhere near at this time of the day, for there must have been close to half a million birds roosting in it, each expressing his and her frank opinion to the other of the state of the environment and the sort of day they had just had. A pair of partridges huddled together under a clump of gorse at the far end but their familiar *Karowick-Karowick-Karowick* evening call was drowned out the moment the hordes arrived.

During the summer a pair of corncrakes took up residence among the tall grass in the drier ground in the centre of the bog, but by this time of the year they were well on their way to their holidays in Asia. In any case, such shy and retiring birds could never have tolerated the racket around them in those autumnal evenings, even the two pair of mallard that habitually nested by the waterside through the summer months preferring to seek pastures new when the rowdy newcomers arrived.

My brother called it the 'Rattling Bog', and he couldn't have given it a more appropriate name.

There were no rabbits in the Rattling Bog. Lang Lugs, the big brown hare, was the only major non-avian resident and even then he only used it for sleeping in during the day in his well-concealed form on the drier ground among the tall rushes. Each night, he would set off on tour, out through the hole in the dry-stone wall that surrounded the bog, lolloping his way through the dockweed and thistles and ragwort in the fields beyond, heading out there towards his distant feeding places, somewhere far out there where the starlit firmament joined the sleeping earth in soft embrace. Or, as the more superstitious of the old people would have it, to join the forces of darkness somewhere out there at the edge of infinity in cabalistic rituals as old as time itself.

My brother was fascinated by the Rattling Bog and, in particular, by Lang Lugs. Geordie was a year younger than me, and probably even more strongly imbued than me with that strange itch to discover what was on the other side of the hill that has made so many of us Scots such inveterate itinerants. I think that in Lang Lugs he saw much of the free spirit that he himself aspired to be, like the 'wild rapparee' of Irish song and legend, an untamed wanderer of heath and machair, a capricious creature shorn of all the irksome responsibilities and cares of humanity, free to roam as and wherever he wished.

We knew where Lang Lugs made his resting place among the rushes of the Rattling Bog, but we never ventured near it, afraid that we would scare him out of the bog for good. He, in turn, became less wary of us, even when, on the rare occasions, we met him in the outlying fields far from his home. There were times when winter floods completely covered the Rattling Bog with up to three feet of water, enforcing upon the hare a temporary flit from the bog to drier ground until the floods receded. This meant that the Old Bog Road was also covered in water, necessitating a very wide detour by us through the fields on our way home from school. Occasionally, at times such as those, we would come upon Lang Lugs out in the fields, sitting bolt upright, nose twitching, ears standing straight up, great pop-eyes regarding us with unblinking curiosity. So long as we stood still, he would continue watching us like this, but the moment we made a move towards him he would be off with an unhurried loping gait, round marble-like eyes jutting from the side of his head, peering back at us as he fled.

Our cottage sat at the southern extremity of the Rattling Bog. My brother came cycling home from the cinema one night, eyes sparkling with excitement, beseeching me to follow him back down the road. I jumped on my bicycle and followed him. It was the month of March and the moon had never been brighter. Geordie uttered not a word to satisfy my curiosity as we pedalled rapidly down the Old Bog Road. We pulled up by the stone structure bridging the burn at the northern end of the bog. Across the bridge from us, the Rattling Bog was bathed in silvery light. Out in the centre of it, little marionette-like figures danced and weaved and bobbed and jostled on hind legs, like moorland pixies in gladiatorial combat. It was a spooky sight, and with the eerie light flickering with ghostly shadows, it took a few seconds for my nerves to settle. There were twelve of them; hares all paired off, boxing each other in that annual saturnalia which had helped give hares a rather sinister reputation throughout the ages, a reputation for associations with the occult among many other things, and had irrevocably damned them with the 'Mad March Hare' epithet.

We knew that Lang Lugs had to be one of the participants before us, for this, after all, was his patch, but we could not distinguish one from the other among the silhouettes on the bog. Most of them were doing nothing more effective than shadow-boxing, just pawing at each other, but one of the two contestants nearest to us had a very professional look to him.

He was giving his opponent a torrid time indeed with his ring-craft: a left cross to the short ribs accompanied by a savage right hook to the liver followed by some murky work in the clinches, and finally a classic straight left to the snoot and a lightening right to the side of the head that sent his opponent tumbling backward among the rushes. 'That was sheer class, real Joe Louis stuff,' enthused my brother ecstatically as we pedalled homeward an hour or so later. 'That just had to be Lang Lugs in action!'

By the time Geordie and I reached our late teens we were deemed competent enough shots to be allowed out with the family gun. This was a double-barrelled twelve-bore shotgun, and it was *old*. The stock had been broken and repaired in the ancient past, and the barrels had been bent and the ends sawn off through a fall on a rocky seashore somewhere or other in its turbulent history. It had so many little brass plates screwed on to it here and there that it looked as though it might have seen active service at the OK Corral under the auspices of Wyatt Earp or Doc Holliday.

It was, I suppose, rather a tatty old thing, if truth be told, something that certainly did not belong in any fancy gunroom, but the important thing was that it was ours. When we had it in our hands, we were kings. To us, it was the most beautiful gun in the world. The stock had a patina to it such as you could never hope to find, we believed, even on the oldest and most expensive Purdey ever made. And the grain of the dark, sleek walnut had such an intricacy of sinuous curls and such a delicacy of turbinations interlaced throughout it that it was sometimes hard to believe that this beautiful timber could have been created solely by the forces of nature.

Patina on wood comes through age and use, and our gun had had plenty of the latter through the generations. Now, it was getting a new lease of life through Geordie and myself, and not just because of our forays in pursuit of game through moor, field and woodland. On wild winter nights, when banshees were moaning drearily in the blackness of the chimney and raggedy old witches were riding broomsticks through the slashing rain about our cottage, daring us to come out and play with them, we would sit by the hearth, taking the gun to pieces methodically, oiling all its parts, polishing it, reassembling it, polishing it again, over and over again, lavishing upon it the sort of care and attention that we would, alas, be unlikely to lavish upon any future girlfriends. Wyatt Earp and Doc Holliday had never taken better care of their weapons than we did of that battered old veteran of ours.

Although we were adequate enough shots, more importantly, we were careful enough gun handlers. The Old Man had taught us to be so, and our father was a very careful man. Always unload the gun, he kept on telling us, before you go through a wire fence or over a dry-stone wall. Never assume a gun to be unloaded until you open it up and check it out. More people are killed by 'empty' guns, he opined, than you could shake a stick at. After laying your gun on the ground for any reason, always open it up before you fire it to ensure that no mud is clogging the muzzle. Never, ever, leave a loaded gun unattended, he would warn, for some idiot was sure to start fiddling with it. Never let the hammers fall on empty chambers, for this would do the nipples of the gun no good at all, and would put extra strain on the springs of the hammer, the locks and the firing pins. In the end, we knew every spring and screw and stud of the gun's mechanism, even if there were times when we felt that the Old Man did tend to go on a bit about it all, for we, with the fires of youth burning impatiently within us, wanted action, not talk. We wanted to get out there into the wide open spaces and start blasting everything that moved.

This, too, was a great big 'no-no' for the Old Man, however. Never point a gun at anything you don't want to kill, he would drill into us, and never, but never, kill anything you don't intend to eat. A man who took pleasure in killing for the sake of killing was nothing but a murderer in the Old Man's eyes, even if the victim was nothing more important in the scheme of things than a common old seagull.

The Old Man's homilies are lessons I remember as clearly today as any biblical commandments our old headmistress ever pumped into us in primary school. Through dear old Jenny Whiteright's teaching, I have so far refrained from worshipping graven images and I have never overtly coveted my neighbour's ass nor his manservant, and through the Old Man's influence I have never yet shot anyone, although I have to admit that occasionally even at this late stage in my life, the temptation can be overpowering.

The 1940s was a dreary period of wartime rationing, and we had permission to shoot over the farmland on which we lived. The farm and its environs were well stocked with game, and the pigeons, rabbits, ducks, greylag geese, and the occasional pheasant we shot were welcome additions to the meagre rations of that time. Sometimes my brother and I would go out on our own with the gun, but more often the Old Man did the shooting while Geordie and I trailed along with him to beat out clumps of gorse, bracken and scrub in order to chivvy out whatever happened to be lurking inside.

Considering everything, it was ironic that it should have

been the Old Man firing the gun when we had the accident. The horror of it is as vividly entrenched in my mind today as when it happened all of those six decades ago.

Geordie and I were beating out a narrow strip of rushes just to the north of the Rattling Bog, while the Old Man stood on the low embankment surrounding the rushes. A cock pheasant exploded from the rushes with the loud, lunatic cackling those foolish birds emit at times like those, straining its wings and body to reach outer space in the quickest possible time. The Old Man's gun roared, the pheasant dropped from the sky and on the far flank of the rushes beyond where I was standing, my brother dropped silently to his knees.

I picked up the bird. Glancing across towards my sibling – whom I had merely assumed to have stumbled on a tussock – I realised that he was, in fact, in serious trouble. He was making desperate attempts to rise to his feet, but he was just floundering around in the mud. I ran over to him. Blood was gushing from a large, circular hole in the back of his head.

I took charge of the situation, for it was not difficult to see that the shock of what had happened had left the Old Man in no condition to take charge of anything. I took off my shirt and ripped a large, makeshift bandage from the coarse cloth. I tied it around Geordie's head to try to stanch the bleeding. Between us, my father and I managed to hoist him, 'piggy-back' fashion, onto my back. Then we began the long trek homeward over field and hill and dry-stone wall. Geordie moaned and gave a convulsive jerk when I stumbled slightly. I tightened my grip on his legs and looked sideways at the Old Man. With a sense of total disbelief, I realised that he was sobbing silently. It was, I think, as great a shock to me as the actual shooting. My father, my great big, tough, unemotional father, was sobbing. This was certainly serious. I lengthened my stride, and George, who was about the same weight as myself, no longer seemed heavy on my back.

We had no telephone in our house to call our doctor in far-off Wigtown and the nearest phone was in a neighbouring farm about half a mile away. I ran over the fields to it. My brother was in bed, drifting in and out of consciousness, when the doctor finally arrived.

'What sort of cartridges were you using?' demanded the no-nonsense old Doctor Lillicoe abruptly.

I dipped my hand into my pocket and fished out a couple of buff-coloured things with 'WD' imprinted on them in black lettering.

'I thought so!' he growled in disgust. 'Fucking War Department cartridges. Black Market rubbish. Useless as tits on a goose. I've had a few other people maimed by those bloody things recently. Take them outside and bury them somewhere. Cheap shit. The bastards who authorised the making of these things should be hung up by the balls in a Turkish fornicatorium.'

He was fishing chunks of purple wadding and pellets of lead shot from my brother's skull as he spoke.

'He'll live, I think,' he predicted when he had finished. None of the pellets have penetrated the bone. Now,' he said to my father, 'you and I deserve a good stiff dram after all that, don't you think?'

But my mother had already produced the necessary bottle and glasses from the cupboard.

'I have never touched a drink in my life, Dr Lillicoe,' she said, 'but now is as good a time to start as any.'

Geordie's wonderful spirit made light of his wound. But it had been a close shave. No blame, thank God, was ever attached to the Old Man for it was quickly established that my brother was nowhere near the target area at the time the trigger was pulled. The bad packaging of the cartridge, the experts explained, had meant that the wadding had been stuffed with pellets when it left the muzzle of the gun, and some weird force of dynamics had made it adopt a downward, wildly spiralling trajectory, with my unfortunate sibling being on the receiving end of it.

He was well on the way to recovery when lockjaw set in. My mother and I visited him in hospital as the crisis approached. I have never been so affected by the sight of anyone lying on a sick-bed as I was while watching my dear brother on that day in Dumfries and Galloway Royal Infirmary. As each violent spasm caused by the terrible disease lifted him bodily from the mattress, I felt as though my own heart was bounding along with his body. Finally, I could take it no longer. I was shaking uncontrollably. I had to leave the room for some respite. I was standing in the corridor when my mother came out. Her eyes were wet with tears. She said: 'I've told him you have been called up for the Army, and he wants to speak to you before you leave for home today.' Fearing the worst, I went back into the room.

His voice was barely audible, and his breath was like the faintest of zephyrs stirring the cotton-grass of his beloved bog. I put my ear close to his mouth.

'When you come back from the Army,' he whispered, 'we'll go the Rattling Bog together. The two of us. Just the two of us. And we'll say 'hello' to Lang Lugs. I promise you that.'

He kept his promise.

CHAPTER THREE

The Road through the Woods

They shut the road through the woods
Seventy years ago.
Weather and rain have undone it again,
And now you would never know
There was once a road through the woods.

Rudyard Kipling

It was a miserable drizzly morning as I cycled up to Kilsture Forest for my first day of work. In Wigtownshire, we called it 'dreich weather'; in other words, typical Galloway weather. I was fifteen years of age, it was November, and there was nothing about this day to indicate that this was to be the start of a lifetime of adventure, happiness and fun for me.

My mother had bought me a shiny new black oilskin coat, leggings and a sou'wester hat for this first day of work, and I sensed that I would be wearing this rain-gear more often than not for cycling to work in the future.

Kilsture Forest was one of the Scottish Forestry Commission's smaller acquisitions, but it was – and still is – one of the more beautiful. It consists of about a square mile of mixed woodland, situated on each side of the motor road linking the villages of Sorbie and Kirkinner. When I started work there in 1945, the eastern section had already been planted with a mixture of conifers and hardwoods. The western half had still to be cleared of scrub in preparation for the planting, and the clearing of it was to be my first full-time job.

Kilsture Forest may be virtually unknown to the outside world today, but seven hundred years ago it was very well known indeed, having been mentioned in a charter granted by King Robert the Bruce in the early 1300s. Being a haunt of deer, especially of roe deer, it became a favourite playground of the Earls of Galloway and their aristocratic friends during the intervening centuries until it was taken over by the Forestry commission in 1934. When I was put to work on clearing the western section in 1945, it was an unruly mixture of every conceivable species of thorn – hawthorn, blackthorn, whins, impenetrable masses of dog-rose and brier, all interwoven with great thick ropes of woodbine. Here and there single trees of birch, elm, sweet chestnut, holly and oak had somehow managed to force their way through, towering like sentinels above the tangle, and a line of ancient, gnarled beech trees demarcated the perimeter. Patches of lime-green bracken and tall, red-flowering fireweed grew profusely throughout all of this, while, in season and at ground level, the rich blue of wild hyacinth, the blush-pink of foxglove and campion and the butter-yellow of primrose added their distinctive splashes of gaiety to the scene.

All of the thorn thickets, unwanted trees and patches of bracken had to be cleared in preparation for planting. This, of course, was long before the era of mechanical tools. Axe, billhook and two-man felling saw provided the *modus operandi* for us back in those days.

There were no such fripperies as industrial gloves during those rugged times and, by the end of each day, my hands would be full of thorns. A good part of my evenings, therefore, would be spent by the fire at home, needle to hand, picking out the thorns. Deep and very painful hacks in the palms of the hands had to be greased with Snowfire ointment to soften them and begin the process of healing, and boots had to be dried out and dubbined for the following day's work. Occasionally, there were worse things with which to contend than thorns and hacks. One day, working dangerously close to a colleague who was wielding a razor-sharp sickle, I got my hand split straight down the centre of my palm between my fingers for my carelessness. The number of stitches involved in sewing my hand back together taught me very little, for youngsters of that day and age were very accident-prone; a similarly careless accident a short time later, this time involving a Yorkshire billhook, nearly removed my kneecap. The fact that the perpetrator in each instance was The Idiot Kennedy did not make me feel any better, for no one in his right senses went anywhere near The Idiot Kennedy when he was armed with a sharp implement.

It was hard, hard work, but we were young and we were tough. I have vivid memories of it all. As I write I can still hear the crackle of burning branches, still feel the sting of woodsmoke in my eyes, can still smell the unique fragrance of each species of branch as their little resin bubbles burst in the heat, wafting their individual perfumes over us. Bushes in which we could see that birds were nesting were left alone, of course.

I discovered a goldfinch nest in the fork of a crab apple tree. The nest was easy enough to find; the crab tree was in full bloom and it was covered by a huge, sprawling dog-rose, also in full bloom. Sitting among the big cream-and-pink blossoms was the cock goldfinch, singing his heart out, his scarlet and yellow plumage glinting prettily among the flowers as he sang. The nest was a lovely little thing of interwoven lichen and birch leaves containing three eggs of the most exquisite light blue with faded-pink dots. We kept watch over that nest … how we kept watch over it! Before we picked up our first tool in the mornings, we checked the nest to ensure that all was well, and our last port of call before we went for our cycles at close of work was the nest. Through the day this beautiful little songster regaled us with his song, a song of thanks, we liked to think, and not even The Idiot Kennedy would have dreamt of disturbing the peace of that little bird and his mate and – later – their three little chicks. When, eventually, they all flew off on their mysterious goldfinch ways, we were sad for a long time.

We were a motley crew. We had, at various times among our squad, a Canadian pilot, a retired plain-clothes policeman, three Timber Corps girls, a Plymouth Brethren Geordie, a professional baker, a test pilot, a rather effeminate dancing-school tutor, three farm labourers, a coal miner, a one-eyed Arnhem survivor, a lobster fisherman, a student teacher, a recently-released jailbird, four Italian prisoners-of-war, and an elderly gamekeeper more renowned for the liquid pungency for his farts than for his expertise in trapping vermin. I spent a whole summer with Farting George, helping him erect a rabbit-proof fence around the perimeter of the forest and I was almost asphyxiated. A miasmic, sulphurous cloud hovered over us wherever we worked and supervisors who visited us periodically to see how we were doing always departed at speed. Environmentalists among my readers should note here and now that global warming did not have its beginnings in this modern era with the toxic emissions of China and the USA. Global warming started in Kilsture Forest, Wigtownshire, Scotland in 1946. Perpetrator – an English gamekeeper called George Pettit living in the village of Garlieston.

Last, but by no means least, we had The Idiot Kennedy.

The Idiot Kennedy was seventeen years of age. I do not know who gave him his *nom de plume*, but he was certainly well-named. The Idiot Kennedy was a born heller. He was a handsome youth with jet-black hair and an incredible appetite for perpetrating the most unpleasant practical jokes. He it was who, while we were resting by the fire in the old cottage in the middle of the woods while the wind and the rain battered against the window outside, threw a couple of 12-bore cartridges, filched from the gamekeeper, into the fire. Ancient cottages are not equipped to cope with this sort of nonsense, and the resultant explosion brought down the wreckage of the chimney and about a ton of soot into the hearth before us. It was The Idiot Kennedy who filled the dancing teacher's Wellington boots with ice-cold water while the owner was toasting his toes by the fire, and it was, naturally, The Idiot Kennedy who nearly knocked out the Arnhem hero's remaining eye with a snowball. If flat tyres were to be found on bicycles as their owners were about the cycle home at the end of a hard day's graft, one always knew where to look for the culprit.

The Idiot Kennedy's day of reckoning came when he made the mistake of mucking about with the lunch-box of one of the Timber Corps girls. Kennedy had been cleaning out a ditch, and from it he had extracted two large and lively eels. Removing the sandwiches from the box, he replaced them with the eels and clamped the lid shut on them. Jen's shriek when she discovered the eels would have awakened the dead.

This time, there was to be no escape for the Idiot Kennedy. With one accord the girls pounced on him and removed every last stitch of his clothing. Having done so, they instructed me to climb to the top of an adjacent, very tall holly tree with his clothing. I could climb like a monkey, so this instruction was no problem to me. I hung his clothes from the topmost branch of the tree. The Idiot Kennedy did not possess any expertise in climbing, and besides, he was stark naked and the tree was very prickly. It made one feel that God was in his heaven and all was right with the world as we lay on our backs by the fire watching The Idiot Kennedy's painful ascent of that holly tree in a biting Siberian wind. His clarion calls each time he spiked some tender part of his anatomy were as music to our ears. The expression 'The mills of God grind slowly...' came inevitably to mind.

There was once a road through the woods. It was, I was informed, a road that linked three great and ancient estates away back in the days of horse and carriage, the estates of Monreith, Galloway House and Barnbarroch. Occasionally, of a Sunday afternoon after church, the families of those days would meet by a small spring in the middle of the woods to picnic and to gossip. In my day the spring was still barely visible, but the road had all but vanished under an accumulation of bracken and briers, the few traces of it to be seen only there because roe deer were using them as tracks.

Sometimes, during lunch breaks, I would slip away from my fellow workers to lie on the little knoll above the spring and daydream, dream about the time long gone when the road through the woods would have been a busy little thoroughfare, when the lords and ladies and their children would gather here with their baskets full of dainty china and comestibles, a time when the laughter of children competed with the happy summer carolling of the chaffinches, when the treetops rang with the joyous sounds of nature and the harsh mechanical racket of this modern era had not yet arrived to disturb the peace.

There is, however, a darker side to the coin, for the Kilsture I knew was always a forest of ghosts. Skirmishing parties from Scotland's intermittent wars occasionally used it as a base, and it was said that sometimes on a clear night the poacher out and about around these parts could see the glint of harness irons and lance heads, could hear the muted clump of hooves as spectral horsemen padded their way along the road through the woods, still out on business that is none of your business or mine.

But perhaps this is simply one of those stories encouraged by the various owners over the centuries to persuade the likes of you and me to stay in our beds o' nights when we might be getting up to a little nefarious business of our own within the dark recesses of Wigtownshire's Kilsture Forest when the hunter's moon is riding high in the sky.

———❖———

Recently, I went back to the forest on a sentimental visit; went back, mainly, to see whether the trees we had planted all those years ago had survived our often cavalier approach to the science of planting. I was pleasantly surprised. The trees were sixty feet high now and thick on the ground. Kilsture had grown again. All visible trace of the road through the woods had gone, buried under a thick carpet of bracken and fallen leaves.

I found the spring, but only one who knew the forest as well as I did could possibly have found it. The water surface was completely invisible, covered as it was with an accumulation of sixty years of dead bracken. But I knew its location, for I had been allowed to plant this knoll myself. I had planted Norway spruce, the 'Christmas Tree' of legend, upon it and, as a marker by the spring itself, a rowan tree. The rowan was a scarlet joy to look at, covered in red fruit, and a bullfinch was gorging himself on them, quite unafraid. I edged my way in under the spruce and dumped my haversack on the thick, soft carpet of leaves under them.

It had begun to rain, a soft, dreich Galloway drizzle. But I knew I would be protected from the elements by the thick, overhead canopy of those friendly trees I had planted myself all of sixty years previously. Tonight, I would sleep well. Also, I had the comfort of knowing that I had a half-bottle of whisky inside my haversack in case the ghosts of the past came a-visiting along the road through the woods.

This time, though, I had nothing to fear from them. Why should I, anyway?

Now, I was one of them myself.

CHAPTER FOUR

Birds with Attitude

The stars grew bright in the winter sky,
The wind came keen with a tang of frost,
The brook was troubled for new things lost,
The copse was happy for old things found,
The fox came home and he went to ground.

John Masefield

I can remember few things in my Scottish Galloway upbringing that affected me as much as did the haunting sounds of the greylag geese arriving from their Icelandic wilderness at the beginning of each winter. Perhaps I should rephrase that for, on reflection, I think that the sounds of their departure affected me even more. I so much longed to join them on their marathon journey, you see.

They came to the Galloway shores during the latter part of October each year, tens of thousands of them, skein after skein of them, each looking for a landing spot among the grey hordes down below. They chattered continuously to each other as they circled. When I was a little boy, I used to imagine their conversations to each other:

'There's old Blethering Jennie down there. She does rabbit on so. She talks about nothing but herself, when I just want to talk about me. Dreadful bore, and selfish with it, too. Hope I don't get stuck with her this winter.'

'Good God, look! Surely that's not that creep Randy Andy down there? He tried to get his wing over me back in Iceland in the summer. You would think he would have had the decency to wait until no one was looking, wouldn't you?'

'Hope the old farmer has left out a better quality of corn and potatoes for us this year. Last year's was a damned disgrace, so it was. I had a good mind to report him.'

'Do you think those bloody shooters will be coming to harass us again this year? I know where I'd like to stick their damned guns.'

'This migration business is just plain daft, isn't it! Why do we have to leave all that lovely Icelandic winter behind for this lousy Galloway climate?'

'Thank God we're here, though. I could fair murder a good feed of good soft Galloway eelgrass.'

It is with a certain degree of shame that I now recall that when I was a lad of fourteen I used to spend hours in a freezing muddy hole on the Bladnoch foreshore armed with the family shotgun, waiting until dawn broke so that I could bag our traditional New Year goose as they winged their way overhead from their night on the sea, heading for some farmer's stubble. A blinding snowstorm was the best scenario for this exercise, for then they flew very low overhead, battling against the snow and the gales.

Sometimes I would be joined by the actor James Robertson Justice in the same hole, for he lived only a few miles away in the county town of Wigtown. I looked forward to his company. He was a veritable fund of very fruity stories, and – more importantly to an ever-hungry young lad – he was always ready to share the contents of his lunch box and offer an illicit nip or two from his hip flask.

Unbelievable as it may seem now to all those film fans who regarded him as being the very personification of the patrician Englishman, he was in fact a very proud Scot. He told me that he had cleaned sewers in London for a living before he became a film star, the perfect training, he maintained, for 'working with all those shites in the film industry'.

Unlike Justice and all the well-heeled wildfowlers I met, I only shot for the pot. From the time I was sixteen years of age and I no longer had to do so, I never lifted a gun to a greylag goose again. I fell out of love with shooting. I think that I simply began to like wild creatures in general too much to feel comfortable about shooting them. Especially wild geese. I started, I think, to develop a bit of a conscience about what I was doing, and to believe that no wild creature that has undertaken such a long and hazardous journey deserved to be shot at when it reached the end of that journey. It would be going too far to say that I stopped shooting altogether, for in my later work in Africa, shooting was often a necessary evil but it would be fair to say that for me, the enjoyment had gone completely out of it.

The Gatehouse of Fleet area is one of the most scenic in all of Scotland, and the Skyre Burn, which runs from its source among the Galloway Hills in the north down to the sea beside the little village of Gatehouse, has got to be just about the prettiest little stream you could find anywhere. I should know, for in 1944 I lived for a year by its tumbling waters in a wooden bothy.

The war was not yet over, and timber of all kinds was still in high demand. There was plenty of the 'all kinds' variety around the Skyre Burn, and my friend Jock and I were woodcutters, working for a timber merchant based in Newton Stewart. This, of course, was long before the era of the chain saw and our tools consisted of six-pound Swedish felling axes and a big manual two-man crosscut saw. Our living quarters consisted of a wooden bothy with over-and-under bunks in a clearing close to the stream. Lighting was by paraffin lamps.

The trees we were felling were not, in truth, up to much in commercial terms and in normal peacetime years no timber merchant of any repute would have given them the time of the day. A few good quality larch and Scots pine were sprinkled among them, however, and I suppose that they made it all worthwhile for any timber merchant who purchased the rights to fell. They were all growing on the hilly ground on each side of the burn, from the main road which ran alongside the Solway Firth to the lower slopes of the Galloway Hills to the north of us.

Before the war, this had been part of a large estate, and the former owners still retained the shooting rights. To protect their game, they also retained old McAllister, their mean-spirited old gamekeeper who lived in a cottage down by the roadside. He had his work cut out with us. The Skyre burn was noted for its sea-trout and pheasants slunk about in the undergrowth all around our bothy. Jock and I, I regret to say, partook freely of them all when the gamekeeper was not around. McAllister was heard to remark with some bitterness one evening in the village pub that we fed better than he did. Living was cheap for two young woodcutters in those days.

The work was hard, but it was a very pleasant time for me. We were free as the air, and being nothing but rather mischievous youngsters, we derived enormous pleasure from winding up McAllister. Winston Churchill had Hitler and Mussolini to contend with. McAllister had us.

Our little clearing was an ornithological paradise. Goldfinches fed on the knapweed, their flickering scarlet and gold a moving kaleidoscope of colour against the purple of the knapweed. A cock bullfinch piped at us daily from the lime-green fronds of a tall, slender larch behind our bothy, his pink breast puffed out with pride at being undisputed seigneur of the neat little nest swaying at the tip of the branch behind him, and his neat little wife sitting on their clutch of eggs. Redpolls and siskins were regular visitors and a rose-breasted linnet nested in the big yellow gorse bush at the far end of the clearing. Larks serenaded our appearance at the bothy door each morning with their endless refrain away up there in the blue beyond. And the joyous carolling of the chaffinch rang out all around us. High over the Galloway Hills a pair of golden eagles soared, and the strange mewing call of the buzzard came faintly to our ears from some distant corrie. Incredibly, a tiny jinking merlin flashed past us one day, going like the clappers, as merlins always seem to do, its body a blur of lavender-blue and delicate salmon-pink. I had been told by a roving hill shepherd that a pair was nesting in the deep heather further up the hill, and this was obviously the male out on patrol.

It was an idyllic setting, and we revelled in the peace of it all. We were completely content. But the highlight of our year was yet to come. It happened on a cold but clear morning at the start of our first winter there. Jock and I were sitting on the step of our bothy, enjoying our first cup of tea of the day and admiring a skein of geese flying low overhead past us, preparing to land on the shore away down below us. Before our startled eyes, a goose planed down to crash-land with an almighty thump about fifty yards from where we sat. We ran over to our visitor and if fluffed up its feather and told us in goose Anglo-Saxon to go away. Normally, it would have made a welcome addition to our daily diet of rabbit and pheasant, but something about its gallus attitude stayed our hand. It made several attempts to take off but it succeeded only in making a lot of ineffectual flapping as it scuttled along the ground before us.

We took it into the little shed behind our bothy to examine it. We could find nothing visible about it to prevent it from flying, and we came to the conclusion that it had been spattered at long range with light shot by some idiot somewhere on its way down from Iceland. Perhaps, we guessed, a pellet had lodged in a wing tendon (a diagnosis confirmed a little later by a veterinary friend who sometimes dropped in to see us.)

For no particular reason that I can now remember, we called our new friend 'Mister McGinty'. He became tame incredibly quickly, sleeping quite happily in our shed o' nights and dividing his daylight hours between waddling around our compound eating grass and whatever else took his fancy, and bathing in a deep pool in the burn.

Mister McGinty became fiercely possessive of his new domain and of us. He saw off the gamekeeper's big labrador dog in double-quick time, riding the terrified animal like a jockey down the hill while stabbing fiercely at its neck with his powerful bill. McAllister's spaniel got very similar treatment, and the gamekeeper himself did not emerge unscathed when he attempted to separate the warring parties.

There was a downside to all this protection, though. The vet's daughter, an extremely pretty girl of about eighteen years of age, took a shine to Jock. That gallant invited her to the bothy for tea and cakes. Mister McGinty was having none of this nonsense. He went for her bare legs like the Assyrian coming down like the wolf on the fold. Eventually, she managed to slam the bothy door shut behind her, breathing heavily, badly scratched and uttering words that no delicately nurtured young lady of that era should even have known. She never returned.

Mister McGinty's fame soon spread. Gangs of little children took to peering at him from behind the rhododendron bushes at the edge of the compound. They soon discovered that Mister McGinty hated children with a passion. We asked McAllister if he could put a stop to the kid's gawking, but we discovered that the gamekeeper's dislike of Mister McGinty almost equalled that of Mister McGinty's for him. A ferocious assault on the children by the goose finally sorted out the problem – a combination of the village policeman and a posse of mothers kept the kids away from us for good.

Once Mister McGinty had sorted out the local children, the gamekeeper and his dogs, and – twice – the local policeman, we were left in peace. Mister McGinty was indeed master of all he surveyed. He flapped his wings more and more often as the summer drifted by, exercising them, but he exhibited no desire to travel beyond the bounds of the compound. He felt safe here.

On the vet's advice, we found an old tin bath and filled it with a mixture of soft cattle food, rotten potatoes and porridge. He loved this foul mixture. We did not allow him to sleep out at nights, for we feared that his very fearlessness would have made him a target for the wiles of the local foxes, but otherwise he seemed to be the most contented goose in all of Scotland.

In the beginning, we would occasionally allow him into our bothy at night, and he would sit dozing contentedly in the corner as we read by the fire, but his house manners left much to be desired and we got fed up of cleaning up the evil smelling mess he left behind him. Eventually, we made a joint decision that a living room was no place in which to keep a wild goose, especially one with such bad manners, so, to his great and very vocal annoyance he was relegated once more to the shed.

Mister McGinty's departure was as sudden and unexpected as his arrival. It was morning in late February, with the first hint of spring in the air. The willow and hazel catkins were out by the side of the burn, and the early primrose was peeking shyly out from its mossy cover up the side of the hill. Jock and I were once more sitting on our bothy step, watching Mister McGinty picking idly at invisible things around his feet at the top end of the compound.

Suddenly, there came to our ears a familiar sound. We looked upward. Coming towards us was a skein of geese, necks outstretched as they cleared the trees along the shore-line, heading for the heavens at the start of their long journey to their nesting grounds in Iceland. Quietly and without any fuss, Mister McGinty launched himself into the air, craning his neck, wings flapping smoothly as he made his way upward to join the others, made his way effortlessly upward, upward, upward, ever upward to join the skein, upward to where he really belonged. He slipped in at the tail end of the skein, and very shortly he and they were only specks on the northern horizon. In a brief heart-stopping moment, he was not even a speck, and the skies were empty of life once more.

It was Jock who broke the silence, for the lump in my throat was too big and too hard for me to be able to say anything.

'Take care of yourself, Mister McGinty,' whispered Jock as we lifted our cups in final salute.

It was the middle of October that same year, and we were outside the bothy cutting firewood for our stove, for the nights had started to get chilly. Suddenly Jock whacked his axe into the chopping block.

'Listen!' he exclaimed.

From high overhead came the unmistakable babble of geese. Wild geese. Greylag geese. The first skein of the year, returning to the Galloway shores for their winter holidays. High overhead they flew, just starting to break up their familiar V-formation, thirty of them, starting to circle now, coming lower and lower as they sighted the sea beyond the trees. Suddenly, when they were little more than tree height, one of them peeled off from the others and came straight down over the bothy, cackling loudly and excitedly, winging its way lower and lower down until it was barely skimming the trees. It did one, two, three, four circuits of the clearing, then, performing a sort of victory roll, it soared off upward to catch up on the rest of the flight.

There was silence as we watched the skein disappear from our sight towards the shore.

'That was Mister McGinty,' I said huskily. 'It had to be Mister McGinty. He came back to show us that he was all right.'

'Even if it was Mister McGinty,' replied the ever-practical Jock, 'which I find doubtful, I think you can rest assured that he wasn't coming down here to show us that he was all right. He was simply checking to see if we had remembered to put any food in his old bathtub. He found nothing in it for him, so we won't see him again.'

Nor did we. Jock was always the pragmatist and I the dreamer. It was an early lesson in life for me. Relationships that become too intense often end in tears, and there is no turning back when they do so.

CHAPTER FIVE

The Spindrift Kid

She appeared before me suddenly, silently, like a water-sprite emerging from the Atlantic spume. She startled me more than somewhat, for at the tender age of fourteen I had still to become used to the sight of stark-naked damsels popping up from the ocean in close proximity to me around those Galloway shores back then in wartime Britain.

She had her clothes secreted in a cleft of the rock from which I had, until now, been quietly fishing for pollack and generally minding my own business. Casually and unselfconsciously, she towelled herself down right there in front of me – supremely unconcerned about the fact that she had ruined my angling for the day and had forever destroyed the naïve illusions I might have been harbouring about the natural modesty of the female of our species.

Her skin was the colour of wild honey, a golden-brown all-over tan that suggested that clothing was not something that adorned her body more often than the dictates of convention demanded. Her hair was black as the raven's wing. Incongruously a little strand of pink sea-thrift clung tenaciously to her pubic triangle, bobbing up and down before my fascinated eyes as she towelled her back and shoulders. Unsure as I was of the correct etiquette, I did not offer to remove it and, regretfully, she did not invite me to do so.

She was the most delightful creature I had ever seen in my life.

Apart from her more obvious physical charms, though, it was her eyes that most caught my attention. They were the strangest eyes, eyes that were emerald green with tiny flecks of amber deep within the green, amber that sparkled as she looked at me. They were eyes that seemed to hold me in a hypnotic trance even when, as now, they gleamed with merriment at my obvious embarrassment.

She was, she told me as she dressed herself, fifteen years of age and her name was Ellie. She was a 'tinker lassie', and she was staying with her parents and siblings in a horse-drawn caravan a short distance along the shore. They had arrived a couple of days ago from 'away up north' for the annual harvesting of the famous Ayrshire new potatoes. She loved the sea, and any spare time she had, she spent swimming or rock fishing.

'In fact,' she offered casting a disdainful look at my new and rather elegant sea-fishing gear, 'I can meet up with you here tomorrow and show you what real fishing is all about, if you like?'

Now I am the sort of person who prefers solitude while fishing, and who likes a background of silence on which to hang my thoughts, and I began to demur. She jumped to the wrong conclusion.

'It's all right,' she said crossly. 'It won't cost you anything, and I won't try to have my wicked way with you. Unless,' she added archly, 'you really want me to.'

I surrendered.

'Okay,' I sighed resignedly. 'But wear some dam' clothes, for God's sake. I was reared decent myself.'

Truth be told, it was not really the fishing that had drawn me to this part of the Ayrshire coastline. I was an adventurous lad, and of an inquisitive and enquiring mind. This was Carrick, long renowned as being a land of seafarers, smugglers and mystery. It was, too, a land of memorable men, men whose names and deeds would be told and retold wherever there happened to be a classroom of children to be entertained by the tales.

The classic folk tale of the raggle taggle gypsies belongs to Carrick's county town, Maybole, for here the laird's wife was wooed and won by Johnnie Faa, king of all gypsies, who rode his horse into the courtyard of the castle one day while her lord was away and eloped with her. In Carrick, Robert the Bruce, one day to be king of Scots, was born. In Carrick, too, Robert Burns, king of all Scots poets, was born.

But Carrick also had its darker side, for on this lovely coastline, in the early part of the 17th century, had lived a man whose story fascinated me just as much as those of the Bruce, the poet and the gypsy king. His name was Sawney Beane, and he was the undisputed king of all cannibals.

The legend of Sawney Beane lives on there to this day. He even had a song written about him. He had his headquarters in a deep cave on the shore some three miles to the north of the beautiful little village of Ballantrae.

There were 46 members in Sawney Beane's family, most of them produced through incest. He solved his own particular version of the credit crunch in a singular way: he butchered every stranger who ventured by his cave. In those days, they were plentiful, for this was adjacent to the Glasgow to Stranraer road, the main road for gentlemen farmers to-ing and fro-ing between Scotland and Ireland.

During the 25 years in which Sawney operated there, it was reckoned that he disposed of around a thousand wayfarers by the time he was discovered. The victims were salted and pickled for future consumption, with any surplus being sold as 'venison', 'pork cutlets', 'spare ribs' and the like to unsuspecting shops in Girvan and Ayr.

It was a lucrative business, for many of the travellers were wealthy. When Sawney and his family were eventually rounded up, bags of gold coins and jewellery were found stored with them. Pickled limbs hung neatly from hooks along the interior walls, and buckets of human 'tripe' sat steeping in vinegar in an alcove to the rear of the cave.

Sawney Beane may have been illiterate, but he was an entrepreneur par excellence in the meat trade.

Ellie was fun to be with. Admittedly, her idea of 'real' fishing was not very original, as it consisted simply of a long ash pole, a hundred yards of brown cotton line, some cod hooks, a large cork float, a lump of lead, and a can of lugworm. But it was effective. Most of the pollack and cod we caught she took away for smoking by her caravan and for subsequent barter around

Girvan. There were rabbits by the million in the whins and rocks around us, and she set snares with the expertise one would expect from a 'tinker lassie'.

She occasionally cooked for me, too, delectable stews of fish and rabbit spiced with secret herbs she had gathered along the foreshore and she sang as she worked, wistful old Irish ballads like *The Pride of Petravore* and *The Stone outside Dan Murphy's Door*. She had a pleasant voice, and it blended harmoniously with the carolling of the skylarks away up there in the clear blue firmament in those enchanted days.

We were lucky: the sun shone upon us for the whole ten days we were together there. The air seemed to crackle with that special electricity you feel when you are young and everything is growing all around you, and the aphrodisiac fragrance of the yellow-flowering whins drowned even the salt tang of sea before us. The trees in the copses on the horizon seemed to stand in a liquid light, and the old moorland cottages, unoccupied, slept in the sun, wearing, weathering, and mouldering away as they had done for the past hundred years.

Each day, as the sun was setting over the Ailsa Craig, and I was brewing up my final billy of the day, Ellie would head off over the moorland track to her caravan site. She wasn't much of a one for social conventions; no 'fare-thee-well' or 'see-you-in-the-morning' type of rubbish. She would simply sling her bag over her shoulder, turn her back on me, and go without a word or a backward glance, and I would watch her small form trudge through the bog myrtle, growing smaller and smaller and smaller, until finally it would vanish altogether in the soft gloaming mists.....

My allotted time passed all too quickly. On my penultimate day a storm blew in from the sea with the rapidity and viciousness that is, alas, to be expected in this part of western Scotland.

A bivouac, such as I had, is virtually useless in such conditions. She it was who first spotted the black thunderheads lowering over the Ailsa Craig on the horizon.

'Quick!' she said. 'Come with me! I know a place nearby where we can be dry.'

In short order, we were in a deep cleft in the rocks a few hundred yards to the south of our fishing perch. The storm was now directly overhead, and the wind howled in widdershins around our shelter. It had suddenly become dark, and, equally suddenly, it had become quite cold.

'Let's light a fire,' I said.

She made no reply. At that moment a tremendous wallop of thunder shook the ground around us and a flare of lightning illuminated the cave with its cold green light. I glanced sideways. She had vanished. I could not believe my eyes. One moment she was there and the next she had vanished. I called out to her, once … twice … three times … There was no reply. Somehow, I sensed that there never would be any reply.

The Spindrift Kid, as I called her in my mind, had gone from my life for ever. I had sensed over the past few days that she was becoming restive. Perhaps the storm was the catalyst that made her decide to return to her own kind, back to the mysterious, roving life of the moorland gypsy.

I hung around for a couple of days before cycling along the shore road to where she had indicated that her caravan was parked. The site was empty of life.

A passing shepherd said vaguely: 'Och, we always have tinks here at this time of the year for the tattie picking. I saw a caravan very early yesterday morning heading up the Girvan road. But God knows where they are now. They're only tinks, ye ken, and they drift like autumn leaves. They'll be back next year, maybe.'

His rheumy eyes peered at me with the insatiable curiosity of the very old.

'Why are ye lookin' for the lassie? Did she steal anything from ye?'

'No,' I said sadly. 'She stole nothing from me. Nothing tangible, anyway. What she took with her, I gave to her willingly, and it's not worth chasing after.'

———◆———

It was to be several years later, while I was on National Army Service in Edinburgh, that I read in a historical magazine about the grisly end of the Beane family. When the reigning monarch, James VI, heard of their deeds, he raided the cave with 400 men and a pack of tracker dogs. The Beanes were taken to Edinburgh to be executed. The men were castrated before the eyes of their women, and their feet and hands were cut off. They bled to death before a cheering populace. The women were tied to stakes and burned alive. All except one, who escaped.

A 'Wanted' notice of the day described her thus:

About fifteen years of age, wiry of body, with long black hair. Answers to the name of Elizabeth. She has strange eyes; dark green with flecks of gold in them. She put a spell on her custodian and disappeared into the woods around the Penland Mills, to the south of Edinburgh. Must not be approached, as she is believed to be a witch. Five gold sovereigns reward for news of her whereabouts.

She was never seen or heard of again.

And so, my dear readers, if you fancy a bit of good, quiet fishing on one of the most spectacular coastlines in all of Britain, you could do worse than try the Ballantrae shores.

I suggest you go in late May. Except for the occasional storm, the weather is usually fairly clement then, and it is a good time for pollack.

Besides, it will be time then for the harvesting of the new potatoes, and you never know your luck.

CHAPTER SIX

King of the Road

'... and come I may, but go I must,
And if men ask you why,
You may put the blame on the stars and the sun
And the white road and the sky!'
Gerald Gould

Although he has been gone from this mortal coil for all of four decades now, you may still hear stories about Snib Scott, the tramp, being bandied around the shaded cloisters of the little taverns scattered around the Machars of Wigtownshire, Scotland, any time you happen to drop in for a cheering pint. Often, as is the way of these things, the stories will be aired with that confident authority almost always assumed by those who could never possibly have set eyes upon their subject in real life. But it surprises me not where Snib Scott is concerned. Snib, so lonesome and mysterious in life, has become a legend extraordinaire in death, and country people are very jealous of their legends. Stories about them live on forever, and you can bet your boots that stories about them will lose nothing in the telling as time goes by.

I was a child attending Garlieston Primary School in the early part of the Second World War when Snib was King of Galloway roads. From time to time our paths crossed when we were on our respective travels, he tirelessly striding along with his distinctive loping gait, I usually on my bicycle.

He was a common sight around the little back lanes of the coastal regions of the Machars in those days, and most people were scared stiff of him. Not that he had any reputation for indecency towards children, or anyone else for that matter. Snib, I think, was perfectly harmless; indeed, with the benefit of hindsight, I think that the reason the old boy rarely spoke to anyone might have been because of a certain shyness on his part.

Most of us, the public, were put off him because he was so Mephistophelean in appearance. He looked as though he would have been a perfect choice for the post of boatman on the Styx, ferrying lost souls over the dark and stormy waters to their eternal perdition. He was a towering figure, about six feet in height, rigid of back as a Coldstream Guardsman, with great long mile-consuming legs. He was as hirsute as a Yeti, with glowing, black ferrety eyes that peered suspiciously out at a hostile world from a dense tangle of jet-black hair. He wore a filthy First World War army greatcoat even on the hottest days of summer, and it was tied around the waist with binder-twine. On really hot days the effluvium from him was that of one who might recently have been an integral part of some unfortunate environmental disaster involving tanks of pig slurry.

Occasionally, while I was checking my trout lines by the wee burn on my way home from school, he would sit down on the grassy bank gazing silently down at what I was doing.

While it would be going too far to say that I ever got to like him much as a result of those brief encounters, I think that in his own quirky way he began to accept me a little. He even began to speak to me, *en passant*. Admittedly, our conversation never amounted to anything more trenchant than, 'Hello, Snib,' and his gruff reply, 'Aye, boy,' but at least it was a slightly more intimate familiarity than that which he normally granted to others.

I was leaning over the road bridge, peering into the deep pool down below me, watching a large, solitary trout idling in the sunlight, his tail barely moving and his gills opening and closing slowly as he awaited whatever tasty morsels might come drifting downstream in the leisurely current. I already had half-a-dozen fine trout hanging from a string before me, but a little boy is never satisfied with what he has already caught when he is out fishing, and I was wondering how to add this beauty to the others when the tramp's tall shadow fell over me.

'Nice string o'troot ye've got there, boy,' he growled throatily. 'They'd be just the ticket for ma tea.'

I shrugged resignedly.

'Take them, Snib, if you need them. I can always catch more.'

Without a word of thanks, or indeed any sort of comment, he took the string of trout and marched off up the road, the fish swinging beside his greatcoat from his bindertwine belt. I looked down into the burn. The big trout had vanished. I lifted my line, threaded a large, wriggling worm onto the hook, and lowered it down into the cool, clear water, where it drifted slowly out of sight under the bridge…

It was two weeks later, at precisely the same spot, that I next met up with the tramp. Having had one of those totally blank days that those of us who seek wily Scottish wild trout all too often get, I was dolefully winding in my line for the day when, like a bad dream, he appeared beside me.

'Never mind, boy,' he consoled me, 'Ye canna aye be lucky.'

He took off his rucksack and opened it up.

'Here!' he said. 'Ye can share my 'piece'.'

He handed me a brown paper bag. I opened it with some suspicion. It contained a massive sandwich composed of two huge chunks of bread of a sort of mottled grey hue, soggy with congealed dripping. I gingerly opened the slices. Nestling in the cold fat, like badger droppings sitting in winter slush, were lumps of slate-blue meat of unidentifiable origin.

'What the hell are these things, Snib?' I queried with a shudder.

'Dinna be sae bliddy pernickerty, boy,' grated the old man irritably. 'They're rabbit kidneys. Best bit o' the animal. You eat it all up, son. It'll put lead in yer pencil.'

I put the package inside my schoolbag.

'Thanks, Snib. I'll eat it later,' I lied.

I hurried up the road, hoping that the eels further up would be less squeamish in their eating habits than I was feeling at this moment.

My next encounter with the tramp was quite unanticipated by either of us. I was hurrying home on my bicycle from a trip to the ancient town of Whithorn. Lightning flickered over the Solway Firth a few miles to the east of me and the air had that sort of cold humidity about it that told me that I'd better seek shelter pretty soon. I was not, however, unduly worried, for I knew that storms at this time of year were not generally of long duration, and in any case I knew that at the foot of this hill down which I was now freewheeling, there was a dense copse in which I could take shelter until the storm blew over.

The first splashes of rain were bouncing on the road when I abandoned my bike and jumped over the stone wall bordering the wood and practically into the arms of an equally startled Snib Scott, who was brewing up a billycan of tea by his lean-to on the verge of the wood.

While I was to find out later that the tramp regarded this shelter as one of his most favoured resting places, I was distinctly underwhelmed. I did not expect gold leaf and lapis lazuli settings, perhaps, but this abode, even for a tramp, seemed a bit spartan. Three very rusty corrugated-iron sheets were propped against the wall, with, tucked underneath them, a mangy old horse-blanket spread over a sort of mattress of twigs and straw and leaves and bracken. A long line of black beetles played 'Follow my Leader' over the blanket and a great hairy brown spider industriously darned a hole in its web in the far corner of the lean-to.

Snib handed me an enamel cup and filled it with scalding tea. The tea was very sweet and of the colour and consistency of Archangel tar. Some pieces of boiled rabbit lay on a section of tin beside the fire. He speared a leg with a small length of fencing wire that obviously substituted for a fork in this bijou residence of his.

'Here, boy,' he ordered. 'Haud this ower the fire and roast it. It tastes better that way.'

The wind soughed through the treetops and I was aware of heavy rain spattering down with it. But we were perfectly dry down here under the dense cover of sycamore leaves, sitting side by side, gnawing away at our rabbit bones, just as, no doubt, the original natives, the dark little Picts, had done around this very place at the beginning of time. It was then that I suddenly realised, with a jolt of surprise, that my old irrational fear of the tramp had gone.

In the distance, church bells began to chime faintly in wet air: Millisle Kirk, a wee church standing on its own by the roadside about half a mile to the west of the seaside village of Garlieston. Snib began to talk. He loved the sound of church bells, he said, but kirks were not for 'the likes of him'. I asked him why, and he told me that once he had tried to join the service of that same church, only to be turned back at the door by a frozen-faced beadle who told him that 'unwashed heathen' were unwelcome in the House of God beside 'decent people'.

Snib was still mortified as he told me about it. He considered himself to be a model of propriety, a man who had never worshipped a graven image in his life, and who had certainly never coveted his neighbour's ass nor his manservant, and here he was being moralised to by this wee scunner Jimmy McGhie, who had put a wee thirteen-year old lassie up the spout and forbye had been caught among the bracken of the Millisle wood abaft Jessie McGowan, the tailor's wife.

'Saw them masel,' he chortled. 'Better nor watchin' Roy Rogers in the Whithorn Picture Hoose ony time!'

It was late afternoon when I finally got back on my bicycle. The sun was sinking in a ball of fire over the horizon. I glanced over my shoulder. The tramp was leaning over the wall, gazing after me. I lifted my hand in silent salute. There was no response from him. I hunched my shoulders and strained at the pedals in the teeth of the strengthening wind.

It was to be quite a few years before I had my next – and final – meeting with the tramp. I was now sixteen years of age and, not having seen him on his usual routes in the intervening years, I had all but forgotten him. My father, a woodcutter of some local renown, had been contracted by a farmer to reduce some very large logs lying around the farmhouse to manageable sizes. The trees had been felled some years previously and, having become so case-hardened through lying in the sun over the years, they were resisting all attempts by saw and axe to do anything with them. My father was the possessor of a blasting licence so, one sunny Sunday morning, we headed for the farm armed with the necessary equipment. Jock, a family friend on demob leave, accompanied my father and myself.

The farmhouse was one of those beautiful old Victorian sandstone mansions you occasionally find in the more prosperous farms of Wigtownshire. The farmer and his family had wisely opted to take themselves off for the day to the town of Newton Stewart, fifteen miles distance, and the whole place was as quiet and peaceful as a Tibetan monastery.

The first few logs gave us no trouble. They were far from the house, down at the end of the drive, and they were of fairly soft horse chestnut. My father introduced us to the principles of blasting, a process so simple that even I had no difficulty in picking it up: a two-inch diameter hole was bored with a large manual auger into the log, the hole was packed with gunpowder, the end of a long fuse was inserted, the whole being tamped down with dry sand to keep it airtight. The other end of the fuse was lit, then everyone ran like hell for cover. The logs, when treated thus by an expert like the Old Man, split neatly down the middle from one end to the other.

Problems arose when we got nearer the house. Now we were among the Big Fellas, colossal, warped old oaken trunks lying sullenly at their moorings in the sun and the wind. They were massive, three to four feet in diameter. At this point, the Old Man decided that he had to obey the call of nature. There was a privy at the far end of the steadings and he headed off in that direction.

He had no sooner disappeared than Jock and I decided to try our hand at this blasting business, so easy did it seem to us. Nearest to the farmhouse was a colossal old butt that seemed to us ideal for practicing on. I took up the auger...

Drilling into that damned log was just about the hardest thing I had ever done in my life. What was more, our troubles were only beginning. We lit the fuse and retired to a safe distance. We waited in vain for an explosion. Either the fuse was defective or the powder had got damp. We had no way of knowing. I drilled another hole and we tried again. Then again. And again. By this time, we were thoroughly fed up. Jock went to the Old Man's satchel and gave a cry of satisfaction.

'Exactly what we need!' he exclaimed, holding aloft an evil-looking greyish-brown stick. 'Dynamite! I used it in Palestine when I was in the Army.'

I would no more have handled that thing than I would have fondled an infuriated Gaboon viper, but Jock was handling it with such bravura that I let him get on with it. The stick was added to the impressive queue of explosives within the log. This time, we did not have long to wait. The aggregate explosion was of nuclear proportions. The tree trunk was blown to pieces, one large chunk and two smaller ones.

They disposed themselves as follows. The two smaller chunks went straight through the plate glass window of the farmhouse drawing room. Chunk Number One crushed the Cuban mahogany centre table flat, on its way to reducing a glass-fronted Georgian walnut cabinet full of occasional china to a hash. Chunk Number Two, deviating slightly from the flight path of its companion, improved a singularly ugly portrait of the farmer's maiden aunt out of all recognition by smashing it full on the face. The third – and largest – chunk, missing the house completely, thundered against the corrugated iron side of the barn about six feet from where Snib Scott was reclining inside among the hay enjoying brunch, creating a huge dent in the barn and throwing Snib's heart, liver and lights into a frenetic farandole of sheer, undiluted terror.

The explosion had not gone unnoticed around the rest of the farm precincts. The old red rooster, engaged in amorous dialogue with one of his harem in the middle of the yard, gave a barnyard version of coitus interruptus by disengaging himself with less than gallant haste and flying off like a partridge for the horizon, moulting feathers copiously en route.

Cyril and Prissie, the two pampered Siamese cats who had been sunning themselves on the back porch, scaled with the ease and rapidity of Nepalese Sherpas the Virginia creeper clinging to the wall of the house, not resting in their ascent until they were safely ensconced on the chimney stack. Shep the collie, chivvying fleas around his private parts nearby, made a valiant attempt to join them, being foiled in his attempt only by getting his left hind foot jammed in a fork of the creeper some distance up the wall.

Snib, convinced that his last hour had come, left the barn like a projectile fired from a bombard, to collide with the Old Man who was emerging in some haste from the toilet behind the steadings where he had been having a quiet smoke and a read at an ancient *Dandy* comic he had found there.

The two men stood before us, the Old Man still fixing his galluses, Snib with bits of hay attached to his person, his eyes popping from his head like organ stops and his mouth opening and closing wordlessly. The Old Man was looking at the wreckage of the window in disbelief. The tramp was the first to speak.

'For Christ's sake, lads,' he said peevishly, 'Have ye nae respect? Dae ye have tae make a row like that on the Sabbath Day?'

Snib left that very day, never – so far as I know – to return to the farm. I did not see him again, for I was soon to be off on my own travels, courtesy of the British Army. In her letters, my mother would send me the occasional report on the tramp, then the reports got fewer and fewer, until finally – nothing. He simply vanished into the Galloway mists as mysteriously as he had appeared in my life, with few to mourn his passing.

When I began this story about Snib, I realised how little I really knew about a man I thought I had known quite well. Who was he? Where had he come from? What was his background? Some research was obviously required, so I contacted the few friends still alive in Galloway who had known both Snib and your obedient servant in their heyday. The answers were interesting, if rather inconclusive.

Tam Kelly, whose family farmed Macharstewart, near the village of Sorbie, informed me that Snib was a member of a large local family, and that he had been an occasional summer worker on the farm in his younger days.

'A good, strong worker then,' recalls Tam, 'until one day he suddenly decided that he had done enough for the farming community, stuck his pitchfork in the ground, and gave the soldier's farewell to all sorts of manual labour forever.'

There are plenty who agree with this version of the Snib story. But not all are convinced. Another friend maintains that there were several Snib lookalikes tramping the roads in those days. In yet another story, the *Scots Magazine* in their August 1993 issue featured a most interesting article claiming that 'Snib Scott' was in fact, one Henry Ewing Torbet, who had worked in Dundee as a banker before suddenly taking to the road and ending up in a cave on the Ballantrae coast, eventually dying of hypothermia in Ayr hospital. A check with the John McNeillie Library in Wigtown produced a very similar story, with the additional information that Snib had been jilted by a girl in his banking years, thus starting him off on his endless travels.

'We get the blame for everything!' remarked Marion Neil, my charming informant at the library desk, with uncharacteristic waspishness.

I am not convinced about the banking story. The Snib I remember would not have recognised an accounts ledger if it had hit him square on his hairy visage. In any case, I remember when I was a child, my grandfather maintained that the tramp was the reincarnation of Robert the Bruce, a monarch who knew more than a little about the byways of Galloway six centuries previously when involved in a serious land-ownership dispute with the English.

Take your pick. You are as much entitled to an opinion as the next person. As for myself, while I would not encourage anyone to subscribe to the fantasies of an old Gaelic mystic like my grandfather, all I can tell you for sure is that, once upon a time in a wet wood in darkest Wigtownshire, I dined with a King, and he was a Scott.

I am a pragmatic person, but the facts surely speak for themselves.

CHAPTER SEVEN

A Surfeit of Spanish Fly

Sexual intercourse began
In nineteen sixty-three
(Which was rather late for me) –
Between the end of the Chatterley ban
And the Beatles' first L.P.

Philip Larkin

The natives of the dark forests of Central Africa called it the 'Pepper Bug', for it imparted a pleasantly spicy flavour to the gravy when roasted, ground into powder, and added to their food. Far to the north, far beyond the burning sands of Libya, the Anglo-Saxon called it Spanish Fly. Here, those love-lorn suitors who were too impatient to be bothered with old-fashioned courtesies such as courting, added it discreetly in powder form to the drinks of their sweethearts in order to speed up the process of seduction a little.

I am no entomologist, and the thing looked a pretty ordinary beetle to me when I first saw it in Africa. It was about

an inch in length, with chitinous wing cases of a darkly iridescent blue hue. I had no idea what it was, but an English friend
who claimed to be an expert on creepy-crawlies told me that it
was a sort of cousin of the infamous beetle known as the Spanish
Fly in the Anglo-Saxon world. The reason, he claimed, that the
forest African never used it directly as an aphrodisiac was that
he and she were absorbing it on a daily basis via the cooking
pot, hence his permanently erectile condition and her eager-
ness to have it away with any man, anywhere and any time.

I could not quite accept this colonial cynicism, for I was
generally eating from the same pot, and I had yet to experience
lust so intense that I required a vast harem of wives to keep
it under some measure of control. Perhaps, I thought with a
sudden frisson of alarm, a childhood digging peats on some
freezing Hebridean moor had done some serious mischief to
my libido? Maybe something vital on me had succumbed to
the permafrost? Perhaps a benevolent God was trying to repair
some of the damage wrought upon me then by dumping me
now amidst the greatest concentration of aphrodisia the world
has ever known? It was a sobering thought.

❖

I was employed at this time as a botanist, surveyor and cartog-
rapher by the great Unilever group of London, and I was
currently working in the Oni River region of Nigeria. Massive,
red-barked ironwood trees towered all around me and, in their
shadow, a copious undergrowth of slim ebony trees. There are
many species of ebony, only a few of which reach diameters
large enough to be considered marketable by the timber trade.
This particular species went by the splendid botanical name

of *Diospyrus sanzaminnika*. The bush African called it the 'Elephant-Bark Tree', on account of its greyish-black hue. The bark was also steel-hard. Sawmillers hated it, for when it was put through the headrig saw, shards of the bark flew around the mill like broken glass, sending everyone around diving for cover. But the tree itself rarely grew to more than walking-stick thickness and around twenty feet in height. At the beginning of each dry season the crown burst into flower, tiny white flowers which released a most incredibly fragrant perfume, one that hung in the air like a thick, cloying, invisible mist. This was the start of the dry season, so the ebony was in full bloom.

We had just completed a long and tiring exercise, surveying a large and malodorous swamp, and I had given the crew a few days off work to clean their clothing and equipment. I had set off along the bank of the Oni River with two of my crew, a compassman called Bilinga and a very young, chattery labourer called, appropriately, Gossip. Bilinga came with me willingly, because he liked fishing. Gossip came not so willingly, for his sole duty was to walk in front, swinging his machete to clear the path of thorny vines and to ensure that if a snake was lurking by the side of the track with evil intent, it would bite him first and not the young Master or the compassman. Labourers were ten a penny, but good compassmen were very precious things in that day and age.

And I considered myself more precious still.

⬥⬦✦⬦⬥

The air was thick with Pepper Bugs. They seemed to be much attracted to the ebony blossom, and the whirring of their wings was almost loud enough to drown out the chattering of the colobus monkeys in the treetops above us. Bilinga told me that Pepper Bugs made the best fishing bait. I put one on the hook, practically gagging on the foul smell it emitted as I did so. Almost at once, I had a five-pound tigerfish on the line, standing on its tail in a thrashing of silver spray on the surface of the purling Oni water.

Disappointingly, this magnificent fish, related to the piranha but more like a cross between the Scottish salmon and the barracuda in appearance, is virtually inedible as far as I am concerned. Its flesh is a veritable minefield of small sharp-pointed, forked bones, the memory of which will remain with you long after they have been surgically removed from your gullet. But the bush African, whose ability to chew his way through almost anything would have been the envy of a Canadian wolverine, had no such inhibitions. When I arrived back at camp with four tigerfish, my crew fell upon them avidly.

The one problem I experienced here, in fact, was the feeding of my crew. The bush African is a very carnivorous creature and although the banks of the river abounded with duiker antelope, bushbuck and water deer, such a paradise of peace was this that I was loath to disturb it by firing shots. Apart, therefore, from a few daft guinea fowl that came screeching around our camp, almost begging for it, my shotgun remained silent. However, the boys were happy to exist on a diet of the wretched tigerfish and the river was teaming with them. I thus had only myself to worry about, and I had better things to do than spend my evenings picking bones from my food and from my long-suffering gullet.

I began to study the fish eagles. I noticed that when they picked up a tigerfish, they dropped it straight back into the water, probably disconcerted by its fierce reaction. Some, I noted, had fine perch-looking fish in their talons. I knew that it was impossible for perch and the supremely predatory tigerfish to co-exist – the perch must have their own haven somewhere downriver. I sent Bilinga and Gossip off to investigate. They returned the following morning and their smiles gladdened my heart.

The 'haven' was far down-river, a vast, rock-encircled pool at the foot of a waterfall. Within five minutes of my first cast into the dark waters, I had my first perch, a great golden beauty of about ten pounds.

We were about halfway back to camp when Bilinga and Gossip stopped suddenly, signalling me to be silent. In the undergrowth about fifty yards from the track, a bull elephant was mounting a cow. We watched his ponderous lovemaking. Not for the first time, I wondered and marvelled that this colossal S–shaped organ of the bull elephant could find its berth with such unhurried ease. His scream of triumph echoed through the trees and sent a whirring mass of iridescent blue beetles rising all around me in clouds, while the cloying aphrodisiac fragrance of the ebony flowers descended upon me like flurries of perfumed snow as I made my way steadily along the forest track towards my tent.

Ahead of me, Bilinga and Gossip began to sing, a high-pitched, tuneless Hausa dirge, while the two golden fish we had caught below the waterfall swung from a thin stick over Gossip's shoulder.

Tonight, no horrible bony old tigerfish for me. Tonight, I thought happily, I would dine on palm-wine and fresh, succulent perch, with lashings of delicious Spanish Fly gravy.

It was not all hell in the tropics, I reflected, provided one knew how to work the system.

CHAPTER EIGHT

The Professor

When I first met him, he was wearing two ties, one red and the other blue and his rolled up black umbrella was perched neatly on top of his crinkly head. His name was Professor Sanderson, he told me, and he was going to his cousin's wedding. He knew that it was the European custom to wear ties to weddings and funerals, so being a man who left nothing to chance, he had put on the only two ties he possessed. Of all his hunter colleagues, he was the only one who was literate, so it was natural that they should have bestowed upon him the title of 'Professor'. It was a title that he wore with dignity and no little pride.

I got to know the Professor quite well. He had been something of a travelling man in his youth, having even spent a couple of months staying with a friend near Leicester, England, a fact which he never ceased to brag about. He was passionate about hunting here in his native Liberia, and the English penchant for fox hunting had made a deep impression on him.

When he got back home to Liberia, one of his first acts had been to gather together every stray dog he could find for hunting expeditions. He called his pack 'the Porn Hunt', and he used them mainly to drive cane rats out of inaccessible thorn scrub to waiting guns.

He invited me to one of those hunts. His pack, I was to find, was aptly named. I had never seen a more wretched collection of mongrels in my life. They fought with each other constantly and, when not fighting, they copulated with each other indiscriminately. I couldn't imagine how the Professor was going to be able to discipline them enough to act in a common cause when it came to hunting. Especially when it came to hunting cane rats, for every dog I ever saw was very anxious to put the cane rat on his menu, and the instinct to kill and eat the creature instantly rather than drive it out to waiting guns was high in every dog.

The cane rat is about the size of a terrier dog, rather like a beaver in appearance and it lives on grasses and sugar cane. It is excellent to eat, and the meat is sold in markets throughout West Africa. Hunting it with dogs is a popular sport; West Africa's equivalent, I suppose, to the English hare-drive.

Somewhat to my astonishment, the drive was a success. The dogs settled down, I did not get bitten, and the Professor and I bagged two cane rats each. That night, at the Professor's house, his lovely wife Mary made us a delicious 'palm-oil chop' with one of the rats, and so much palm-wine was consumed that Mary deemed it wiser for me to sleep overnight at their house.

><><><><><

I was at a bit of a loose end around this time. My contract had expired, and I was looking for one last job to do before I took my leave. A friend of mine at the time happened to be Cecil Dennis, the Minister for Foreign Affairs in the Liberian Government. We met at Christina's Bar, a Spanish drinking spot much favoured by the avant-garde of Monrovia.

'I think I may be able to help you, Don,' he said. 'Our Game Department are hoping to set up a reserve of about five hundred square miles over by the Cavalla River on the Ivory Coast boundary, but they would like to have some idea of how many species of wildlife exist there now. A sort of feasibility study, if you like. I have suggested that you might be interested in doing a complete survey of the area; topography, vegetation, wildlife, and so on. If you accept, you have about six months in which to complete it. Pick your own team.'

I was delighted. So was the Professor, for I appointed him without hesitation as my amanuensis and general factotum. Within the week we had everything loaded into our truck, ready for the long journey across country to Cape Palmas, our base.

Even at first sight, it looked to me ideal country for the establishment of a nice little game reserve such as that envisaged by my employers; the right mixture of open grassland, orchard-savannah, pockets of large mahogany trees, thorn-scrub and streams. The Professor selected his team from local 'bushmen' and hunters, and we were off and running. We camped out, moving our tents as we completed our survey in each section.

We lived very much off the land, buying yam and cassava and palm oil from the subsistence farmers around the area, and shooting such guinea fowl, francolin and antelope as we required. Catfish – horrendously ugly, but surprisingly tasty – were in abundance in the Cavalla river, requiring little effort to catch. Old abandoned farms, of which there were plenty hereabouts, all had smatterings of fruit trees on them, giving us a plentiful supply of oranges, lemons, guavas, bananas, mangoes, avocados, grapefruit and so on. Pineapple and groundnuts were also there for the picking. We fed like kings at very little cost. 'Wine trees' were scattered around wherever we looked, so the workers were kept happy with ample supplies of palm-wine for their nightly concerts around the camp fire. It was good to be alive.

As for wildlife, there was plenty of that, too. Elephant and buffalo tracks were all over the place. On a little tributary by the Cavalla I saw my first pygmy hippopotamus, and we spotted a beautiful sitatunga antelope in a patch of wet ground. We came upon an aardvark hole, and scratches on numerous trees indicated the presence of a large leopard. Bushpigs rooted among the abandoned farms and fish eagles patrolled the skies.

By our campfire in the evenings the fairy flycatcher – surely the most beautiful and most approachable of all birds – flickered before us in a delectation of hazy blues and silvers. The Professor remarked to me that he would like to build a retirement home right here for himself. I knew the feeling, for I could think of worse spots in which to end my own days.

✕✖✕✖✕✖✕

The time passed all too quickly and within a month we would have completed our survey. The Professor and I were passing through a grove of stilt-rooted trees in a patch of wet ground by the river. A small brown body shot out from underneath some stilt roots at us, snarling ferociously. The Professor, after one horrified glance, gave a yelp of terror, dropped his gun, and went up a nearby fig tree like a squirrel. In the African jungle, when your guide reacts instantaneously to any emergency, you don't hang around to wonder why. You follow him with all due speed. It is one of the first lessons you learn in the forests of the White Man's Grave, and it had saved me from much unpleasantness in the past. The fig tree was easily climbed, a mass of branches from head height upward, and seconds later the Professor and I were jostling for position on the topmost branch.

'What the hell was that thing?' I asked breathlessly.

'A honey-badger,' replied the Professor.

The honey-badger, or ratel. Just about the most ill-tempered creature in all of Africa. I had heard of it, but this was my first encounter with one. Although about the size of a European badger, it would attack anything, up to, and including, the mighty elephant and buffalo. Our specimen was now sitting on its haunches, glaring up at us, daring us to come down. I had no intention of doing any such thing, and neither, quite obviously, had the Professor.

'Why the hell did you drop your gun?' I asked irritably.

'Because I needed both hands for climbing,' he replied with some asperity.

'What in God's name made it go for us like that?' I wondered.

'It's a female,' said the Professor, 'and I think she has got young ones among the stilt roots behind her. You can't blame her. She's only protecting her family.'

'Is that so!' I said with heavy sarcasm. 'How long, may I ask, is that brute going to keep us treed up here while she protects her bloody family?'

'Probably only a few hours,' he replied soothingly. 'Eventually her maternal instincts will take over and she will go back inside to feed them.'

'Great!' I said witheringly. 'So all we have to do is sit up here twiddling our thumbs until that bundle of spite's better nature takes over. That could be forever, for she looks to me as though she doesn't possess a better nature.'

'Have you got any better ideas?' asked the Professor coldly.

'Yes,' I said. 'I've just had one.'

He looked at me with some suspicion.

'I will keep her occupied,' I explained, 'by throwing bits of wood down upon her from this front side of the tree while you climb down the back and attack her from behind. During the commotion, I can make my escape and bring back help for you.'

'I beg your pardon?'

I could see that he was a man with no sense of adventure, and that he needed some encouragement.

'Come on now,' I said. 'You're a famous hunter. It should be easy for a man of your calibre.'

'I am also a cautious hunter,' he pointed out, 'which is why I am still alive.'

'You've shot elephants. You're surely not afraid of a little thing like that.'

'I had a gun when I shot elephants,' he reminded me unhelpfully. 'And there is nothing little about that animal. Look at the muscles on her back and shoulders. Above all, look at the size of her teeth.'

I had to admit that he had a point. As if to demonstrate the validity of his argument, the honey badger had found a tree branch and was attacking it with the utmost ferocity. I couldn't help noting that although it was a good stout branch as branches went, it was being reduced by the honey badger's teeth with disturbing ease and rapidity to a hash of splinters.

It was a long afternoon, and during it I discovered that I was not cut out for arboreal life. Savage fire-ants came in their legions to test whether I was edible. The sun blazed down upon us, blistering our skin, and clouds of tsetse flies and horse flies added to our misery. An itinerant mamba about seven feet long came to inspect us and, not much liking what it saw, slid off disgruntled. The end was long in coming, but come it did at last as the evening shadows began to fall over our roost.

How it happened, I do not know to this day. I suspect that one of the honey badger's claws got entangled in the trigger guard of the shotgun lying on the ground while she was examining it for clues. Whatever it was, the gun went off like the crack of doom. The honey badger did a complete backflip in shock, and disappeared into the forest to consider the events of the day. Thankfully, we climbed back down to terra firma, picked up the shotgun, and made our way to camp.

We finished our task within the allotted time and I handed in my report, satisfied that we had done a good job. This story does not, however, have a happy ending. A couple of months later, a murderous little army NCO sparked off a military coup in which the president of the country was brutally slaughtered in his bed and the entire cabinet, including Cecil Dennis, were tied to posts on a Monrovia beach, then, filmed by the world's media, were shot like dogs. The 'Redemption Day Calendar', issued by the new military leaders at the end of the year, reached a new low in world politics by featuring each cabinet minister tied to his post after the execution and drooling great gouts of blood and gore from his mouth.

Vade in pace, Cecil Dennis.

The proposed game reserve never came to fruition. A Lebanese timber man paid a huge backhander to selected individuals within the new regime. A few weeks later the chainsaws moved into the area, and the animals were shot for food and for fun.

As for the Professor, he too came to a sticky end. An important hunter had died in Grand Gedeh County, in northern Liberia. On such occasions, it was customary for hunters to gather from all over the land, drink themselves stupid and let loose with their firearms to see his spirit off to the next world.

The Professor's gun was very old and past its best. The barrels were paper-thin with use, and the locally-made cartridges were quite appallingly dangerous, filled as they were with ball bearings, shards of old iron cooking pots, stones, nails, and any kind of miscellaneous debris. The barrels on the Professor's gun just couldn't take the strain. They burst, and the Professor was decapitated. He was easily identified, my informant said, for although he had no head, he was wearing two ties around his neck.

One red, and the other blue.

CHAPTER NINE

Dr Emmanuel Death

For a short time in the early 1950s I was a near neighbour of Dr Death, and I got to know him quite well. I was conducting a tree prospection in the vicinity of the village of Igbatoro, in Nigeria's Western Region, and Dr Death had his surgery on the outskirts of the village. A large wooden board affixed to a mango tree outside his hut proclaimed in vivid red lettering:

Dr Emmanuel Death Ltd
Specialist in:
Yellowing of Liver and Anus
Sasswood Poisoning
First Class Gonorrhoea
and Working Class Gonorrhoea

I suffered, thanks be to God, from none of the good doctor's litany of horrors, so I had no need to seek his services on a personal basis as yet. But I should certainly have dropped in on him eventually, for I had always been interested in African medicines and the murky world of the witchdoctor. Eventually, I ran into him drinking in Madame Sarah's International Bar.

Madame Sarah's International Bar was a rambling mud hut, roofed with rusting corrugated iron, in the centre of the village. It contained an ancient paraffin refrigerator for cooling the bottles of beer, an iroko-plank bar, three tall mahogany stools, a gramophone, and half of an oil drum serving as a spittoon over in the corner. Apart from the beer, Madame Sarah sold an incredible mish-mash of stuff: Manchester-made machetes, candles, five-gallon drums of paraffin, bottles of red palm-oil for cooking, balls of string, bunches of tobacco leaves, matches by the half-dozen sticks, bolts of brightly coloured cloth, pencils, children's exercise books, tins of pilchards in tomato sauce; in fact, just about anything that would make a penny. An old Irish Catholic priest dropped in for a beer sometimes on his periodic official visits to the area, hence, I suppose her main justification for the 'International' appellation.

Today, the only customer apart from myself was a tall, rather distinguished-looking, grey-haired African who instantly held out his hand to me.

'Dr Death, sir,' he introduced himself courteously.

He was delighted to meet a British subject, he said, for he had spent some happy years as a medical orderly in the Royal Navy, helping cure the interesting ailments suffered by the mariners. His Chief Medical Officer had been a Scotsman called McCorquindale, who drank enormous quantities of whisky and swore at him all the time. The Chief Engineer had been a Welshman whom everyone called Mr Taffy, a man of ambivalent sexuality who also swore at him a lot. Mr Taffy, when in his cups, would try to lure him into his cabin o'nights for 'fun and recreation' assignations. Sometimes, he said, he would accept, for it helped to pass the time on long sea voyages. Dr Death asked me if I happened to be of that persuasion and I thought he looked a trifle disappointed at my firmly negative response.

He cheered up, though, when I suggested that I might be able to put some medical business his way. I had in my employ some three dozen trace cutters and tree prospectors, some of whom would no doubt fall ill from time to time. For an arranged monthly fee to him, I offered, I would send the sick and malingering to him for examination and treatment.

'But no parrot feathers and bat shit and stuff like that,' I insisted. 'Just standard European medicine, that's all. And if any of them come to you with a dose of the clap, I want to know names, so that I can talk to them about the error of their ways.'

I bought him a drink.

'One thing is puzzling me,' I ruminated. 'What is the difference between First Class Gonorrhoea and Working Class Gonorrhoea?'

Dr Death had a twinkle in his eye.

'Nine Nigerian shillings,' he said succinctly.

'I beg your pardon?'

'Nine shillings is the difference. The ordinary working man prefers native medicine. Yes, the bat shit and parrot feathers sort of stuff. I deliver a small incantation with it, and bob's your uncle. I charge him a shilling. Those of higher social standing lower their trousers and get a shot of penicillin up their bums. Then I hold out my hand and say: 'That will be ten shillings, massa.' It comes to the same thing in the end, for both go home happy.'

He paused, then, anticipating my next question, he said: 'and, yes, generally both do get cured, for the one who opts for the native medicine believes in the efficacy of it. It is a thing called faith, and you, as a white man, should know that faith is a very potent force. After all, it keeps you lot going to church every Sunday to worship a hippy who stated two thousand years ago that he was born of a virgin mother to someone who was not her husband, a hippy who stated that he, nevertheless, had come to save the people of this world from their sins, a hippy who was eventually lynched for sedition...'

He stopped to catch his breath and I bought him another beer to cool him down, for it was obviously a subject about which he had strong feelings.

'Come to my little place when we have finished this beer,' he invited, 'and you can see my working quarters. My wife will cook something for you. And don't look so worried. She won't cook anything not suited to the delicate palate of a white man!'

His house was, in fact, quite large and surprisingly well appointed inside. His wife was a slim, good-looking Yoruba, shy at first with me, but gradually opening up under my banter. She had been a nurse at the hospital in Benin City a hundred miles from where we now were, and there she had met Dr Death, who was employed as a consultant in native medicines there. Now that he ran his own practice in this village, she said, she quite often helped him at busy times with injections and the dispensing of medicines and such like, but she never had anything to do with native medicines, nor had she any wish to know anything about them. In any case women were never allowed to become witchdoctors.

Dr Death showed me into his two surgeries. Each had a small sign nailed to the door. The room marked 'First Class Surgery' was as neat and clean as any dispensary one might have found attached to any good hospital anywhere in the world. However, the one marked 'Working Class Surgery' was, for me, the most interesting. Shelves of animal skulls lined the walls, from those of tiny, shrew-like creatures, to a large, human-like skull which I presumed to be that of a chimpanzee, a common enough animal in the surrounding forests. Little jars containing sinister-looking potions cluttered up his working bench, a shrivelled hand, presumably – and hopefully – from some species of monkey, was nailed to the door and beside it hung a black, hooded cape covered with red chevrons.

'My official garb for the Working Class patients,' he explained.

'I wear the standard white cloak for the First Class ones.'

Behind the Working Class surgery was a tiny room which had a single bed for use by, he said, patients who had to be detained for observation for any length of time.

I was much impressed by the orderliness of it all, and left thinking that, should the need ever arise, I would not object too strongly to finding myself as a patient in the hands of Dr Death, First Class or otherwise.

I was living out in the forest under canvas with my workers, so my opportunities for coming to the village were limited to about once monthly, when I passed through on my way to the Benin bank to collect my workers' wages. I saw very little of the doctor, therefore, for the next few months. I did receive a flurry of medical chits from him, commenting – in generally acerbic tones – about workers I had sent to him with a variety of complaints.

One, I remember, read:

'Ben Akoh. Malaria complainant. This man is a skiver. He has no more got malaria than I have got a white arse.'

And another: 'Johnny Doe. Sore back, he says. Rubbish. This ape gave me a load of cheek when I refused to give him medicine. Feed him to the crocs.'

And yet another: 'Isaac Wilson. Sore finger, alleg-edly. He gives me a sore head. It is buggers like this that give we Africans a bad name. What he needs is a good kick up the gluteus maximus.'

The first time I called to see him in order to pay him his fee, I spent the night in the bed in his Working Class Surgery. I asked him about the 'Sasswood Poisoning' part of his qualifications.

'Oh that!' he said. 'Well, you will remember that recently there was a whole string of murders along the West African coast involving sasswood poisoning which led to the hanging of a prominent politician? Well, the Nigerian Government got so worried about it all that they appointed me as their voodoo specialist at trials. You are an old hand out here, and you are a forester, so you probably know about our infamous sasswood?'

I certainly did. In fact, I had been brought up on boys' adventure tales on the horrors of sasswood in papers for young-sters such as *The Hotspur* and *The Rover*, never thinking for one moment that I would one day be working among forests of the trees that produced the poison. The legendary poison is extracted from the sasswood tree, or *Erythrophleum*, to give it its Sunday name. It was always a tree of the darker and wetter forests, a tall dark-barked, dark-leaved, rather gloomy tree, that always looks as though it might have something nasty about it. We had any amount of it around this area, and there had always been a steady demand for its poisonous properties via the Benin markets. Its timber, too, had always been in demand on the European market, being popular for decorative parquet flooring and the like.

'Trial by Ordeal' had always been a favourite way around the West African interior of deciding an accused man's guilt or innocence. The basic principles of the Ordeal were simple. The accused was put on public trial, and anyone who wished to do so could come and see him. He was made to drink a mugful of the stuff. If he died, he was guilty, and if he was innocent, he lived. I once saw someone die from sasswood poisoning, and it is not an experience I wish to repeat.

So far as I know, no one had yet been able to do a proper analysis of the poison. All, however, are agreed that it is completely lethal. The ones who recover are those who drink it down rapidly. The stomach rejects the horrible mush, making the accused vomit it up. The ones who die, knowing, perhaps, that they are guilty, drink it down slowly and reluctantly, allowing the digestive system to absorb it.

It is rough justice, of course, but the spectacle always brought thousands in their best dresses to witness. It was, I suppose, the African rainforest equivalent of the Epsom Derby, insofar as spectator pleasure went.

This was the height of the dry season and the forests around us throbbed with life. It was a joy to be alive in this primaeval setting. I tried to give my workers each Sunday off, so that they could rest up or go off to the village to buy bits and pieces from Madame Sarah or sample her beer. On such days I would wander off on my own through the trees, to sit by a little stream ten miles from our camp, just listening to the soft, soporific tinkle of the water over moss-encrusted stones below me, and, above me, the tuneful call of little sunbirds and the high-pitched metallic call of lovebirds in the treetops.

Once, a pair of lovebirds landed on a thin branch just above my head as I lay on my back on the bank. They paid not the slightest attention to me, for they had eyes only for each other. Their olive-green bodies and roseate heads gleamed in the afternoon sun and they twittered love things softly and endearingly to each other. They began to walk sideways along the branch, keeping their bodies tight against each other, walking step for step so as to maximise the feel of their bodies against each other, pausing often to kiss. They were besotted with each other, and I dared not move a muscle for fear of disturbing their love fest. I plead guilty to having more than a trace of anthropomorphism about me, but surely no one who saw those little birds as I did on that day could have doubted that some, at least, of God's wild creatures are capable of falling in love.

Once, I came upon a large male leopard sunbathing on the bank of the stream. He was on the opposite bank, eyes closed, but he was well aware of my presence. He opened one drowsy eye and looked at me with sleepy, incurious gaze, as though to say: 'Why don't you just go away and leave a chap in peace?' I sat down ever so carefully. He closed his eye and continued to pursue his mysterious leopard dreams. I could have sworn that I detected a contented little smirk on his face.

The forest, unfortunately, contained plenty of less pleasant creatures, and one was about to give me a most unpleasant fright. My senior tree-finder, a lad called Délé, was working his way slowly through a tangle of vines and thorns about twenty yards behind me. I heard a loud scream and spun round to see him fall to the ground with seven feet of infuriated black cobra attached to the calf of his leg. By the time I got to him, the reptile had disappeared into the bush at high speed. I immediately applied the cut-and-suck remedy to his leg and then put a light tourniquet just above the area of the bite.

I knew that we had to get him to Dr Death quickly, for cobra venom is very fast-acting and extremely potent. While I was working on the lad therefore, the rest of the workers were constructing a litter of sticks and vines with which to carry him. We then set off at a jog-trot out of the forest, with me praying all the way that Dr Death had the appropriate anti-venom in his surgery.

By the time we got to the village, the leg was swollen like a football and it showed a horribly mottled tartan of blacks and blues and greens on the lad's light-hued skin. Dr Death looked grave.

'How long since he was bitten?' he asked.

'Half an hour ago,' I replied.

'Well,' he said, 'I'll do my best, and I do have anti-venom here but I have to warn you that I have no time to check whether he might or might not be allergic to it. So, this anti-venom could very well kill him on its own. But it's an emergency, so I'll just have to take a chance on it.'

Dr Death was sweating freely as he filled his syringe.

The lad was sleeping fitfully when I left him.

I called early next morning. Dr Death was still trembling visibly, but he was smiling.

'He had quite a good night,' he said, 'and I'm sure he'll recover. If he was going to die, he'd have done so last night. Cobra victims either die quickly, or they recover quickly and suffer no ill effects. He'll be okay now.'

'You don't look so good yourself,' I said.

'I was awake all night, watching the patient,' he admitted.

I took him by the arm and said: 'Okay, now let me be your doctor. I have some medicine that will help you.'

I sat him down in a chair and produced a bottle of Glenfiddich whisky. I poured him a good stiff dram. He began to laugh.

'You Scots are an amazing race,' he chortled. 'You despise us witchdoctors, yet you are the best witchdoctors going yourselves. A bottle of that stuff in your pockets, and you are Kings of the World.'

I clinked glasses with him.

'Well,' I remarked, 'Even an old cynic like you would have to admit that it tastes better than bat shit any day.'

I left the area soon after, not to return for another couple of years. There was a new road into the village by then, and Dr Death had gone. His house was now a Wesleyan school, and little children in blue uniforms wandered aimlessly about. The International Bar was still there, however, and there was one customer, an elderly white man.

'Father O'Banion,' he said by way of introduction. 'I didn't meet you last time you were here, but I heard about you from Emmanuel Death.'

'What happened to the old rascal?' I asked.

'Actually, I met him a little while ago in Lagos,' said the Father. 'He has given up the medical business, and he now publishes a magazine for the lovelorn called *Sex With Daisy*. I read it once and it is pretty hot stuff. So hot that I didn't understand much of it myself.'

His old eyes twinkled roguishly.

'I'm old-fashioned,' I said. 'I liked the old days better. Let's drink a toast to the Dr Emmanuel Death we knew and loved here.'

'And to his First Class Gonorrhoea and his Working Class Gonorrhoea,' the Father reminded me. 'Let's not forget that.'

'Amen to that, Father O'Banion,' I said.

CHAPTER TEN

Always Something New

It was Pliny the Elder who famously wrote 'Ex Africa, semper aliquid novi.' The film star Clark Gable said something similar while filming with Ava Gardner and Grace Kelly on that great continent in the middle of the 20th century.

His Latin being a bit rusty, what Mr Gable actually said was, 'Where the hell did all these goddam flies come from?' But then one should, I suppose, expect a certain degree of loucheness from one who, reputedly, steeped his false teeth overnight in bourbon, to the palpable distress of those starlets who were forced to exchange romantic kisses on set with the heart-throb at crack of dawn.

I have never claimed the erudition of the great Latin scholar or the rugged good looks of Mr Gable, nor had it ever been my good fortune to share any part of Africa with the delectable Misses Gardner and Kelly. But I *can* claim certain bragging rights over the lot of them: I was in Africa longer than they, and once upon a time I was accorded the privilege of being the Guest of Honour at a pygmy shindig in the heart of the rainforest.

◎◎◎◎◎◎

Finding your first pygmy encampment is not, as the reader might understandably suppose, the greatest difficulty experienced by the traveller who wishes to see what the interior of Africa is all about. Getting permission to enter that benighted continent in the first place can seem to be an almost insurmountable hurdle. (Although a suitcase full of greenbacks can help your cause immeasurably.) The first-time visitor could be excused for thinking that African officials are hell-bent on ensuring that whites stay right where they belong – back home by their own firesides. To ensure that as few tourists as possible come out to corrupt their pristine shores, they have fine-tuned the art of petty bureaucracy to the nth degree. Many years ago, on my first visit to Liberia, I was asked to fill in a form that contained the following questions:

1. Do you intend to assassinate the Head of State? (If answer is affirmative please state where and when.)
2. Has your father ever been trained in rogering?
3. Have you every been convicted of harlotism?
4. Are you male or female?
5. Why?
6. If unable to read or write, explain why in triplicate on the form provided.

Fortunately, a twenty-dollar note pressed into the greasy palm of the official concerned saved me the necessity of having to answer this absurd rubbish.

It was only afterwards that I realised that this was really what it was all about – money. Certainly that official looked the fattest and most contented immigration man I had ever encountered.

◎◎◎◎◎◎

By Liberian standards, Cameroon officials were models of integrity and efficiency. Nonetheless I was glad when I got clear of the airport. I have never attempted to take anything illegal through customs barriers in my life, but for some inexplicable reason I always have a vague feeling of guilt when having to pass through them, whichever country I happen to be trying to enter. I always seem to be the one selected to be strip-searched.

This was my gateway to pygmy-land. In Douala, I was met by Kamara, who was to be my mentor for the next couple of months during my visit to the deep, dark forests around the Sanagha River. The Cameroon government, with a view to creating a reserve here, had asked me to conduct a preliminary survey of trees, plants, animals and – particularly – pygmy families living in those vast and largely unknown forests.

Kamara was of the great Fulani nation, those tall, aristocratic cattle drovers from the savannah lands to the north of the rainforests. Each dry season, they herded their strange hump-backed cattle hundreds of miles south over the red laterite roads to the cattle markets of the coast for sale. Every so often, Kamara would take a holiday from his herding to wander around those steaming southern rainforests, hunting and fishing. Once I asked him why anyone in his right senses should wish to abandon the crisp, clear air of the cattle trails for the heavy, sticky humidity of the rainforest. He responded with typical dry humour.

'More adventure and variety in the bush, patron. When you're walking behind cows day after day, one cow's arsehole starts to look very much like the other's. Besides, when you're constantly on the cattle trail, girls are hard to come by. They like a slightly more ordered way of life. And they get tired of lovers who smell of cow shit all the time.'

He spoke pidgin French and I spoke pidgin English, the perfect combination because, so I had been told, most of the members of the various pygmy families scattered throughout the forest spoke either one or the other. He instantly accepted my invitation to join me in my forthcoming survey.

I hired a 'bush taxi' for our trip, a wooden-sided French rattletrap of a thing which stank horribly of ancient diesel fuel and even more of ancient goats. Twenty-four bone-shaking hours later it regurgitated us at 'Jacob's Camp,' a sweltering settlement of a dozen mud huts on the fringe of the rainforest. It was to this dismal hamlet we were told that the Baka pygmies came out of the forest periodically to exchange their 'bush meat' and wild honey with the African villagers for bananas, yams and bits and pieces of clothing. (The pygmies did not cultivate anything, but many were already adopting some of the ways of the outside world such as the wearing of 'proper' clothing, as they themselves referred to the tacky trash manufactured in the USA and Asia which was finding its way into even the most remote markets of the African interior.)

We briefly toyed with the idea of making this hamlet our temporary base while we got ourselves organised for our trek into the interior and, indeed, Jacob, the rascally old village patriarch offered to hire us, at enormous cost, a room in one of his huts. The sole piece of furniture within consisted of a rickety metal bed with an ancient mattress covered in urine stains. It was also infested with bed bugs. Cockroaches scuttled over the floor before us like a sea of black lemmings, and a colossal green spider glowered hatefully at us with hard hangman's eyes from a yellow web in the far corner. Kamara gazed around in disgust.

'My cows, patron,' he stated emphatically, 'would refuse to stay even one night in this horrible place.'

Without further ado, we moved our gear a few hundred yards out into the forest and pitched a tent.

From the point of view of personal comfort, the move was a necessary one, but as an exercise in *entente cordiale* it was an unmitigated disaster. Old Jacob was outraged that we should have spurned his beautiful hut to camp out in the forest, and he set out to make life as uncomfortable as possible for us. He would not allow his villagers to sell us bananas or yams or cassava, or indeed anything at all, and gangs of youths peppered our tent nightly with stones, making sleep virtually impossible. I sat out for a couple of night firing shots over their heads with my shotgun, but this bought only temporary respite. In any case, it was not in our interest to antagonise the locals, and in the end I was forced into doing what I should have done in the first place – give Old Jacob a substantial sum of 'protection money'. Thereafter, we were left in peace, and our relations with the old bandit improved considerably.

At about twice the going rate, I managed to hire from him a dozen of his villagers to carry our gear into the forest. The nearest pygmy camp was reportedly about a day's trek away. I was just pleased to get on my way and out of Jacob's mercenary reach.

It was easy walking. The footpath was narrow but clear of vines, and it was relatively cool in the shade of the towering mahoganies. We had not travelled more than about a couple of miles when we came upon a clearing in which sat an old mammy tending her cooking pot. She hailed me genially: 'Young man, have you eaten yet? No? Well, sit down here and share mine.'

I did as she commanded. Kamara carried on with the porters, saying as he departed: 'We'll rest at the next stream of good drinking water until you catch up with us.'

Her name was Lucy. She was jet black, and of about the cubic capacity of a palm-oil tanker. She was full of fun. She had had six husbands, she said, all dead now through over-use.

'Not a bloody man among them!' she commented somewhat caustically.

She was on the lookout for another one.

'You look a very fit young man to me,' she said, eyeing me meditatively. 'I have never had a white man before but I would be happy to take a chance on you.'

'Good Lord no, Lucy!' I exclaimed in horror. 'Don't even think that way. I would make the worst possible husband. I am nothing but a hopeless wanderer. Besides,' I added, casting my eye over her vast frame, 'a fine, fine looking woman like you, you need a man who will be gentle in bed with you and treat you like a lady. I would get power too much for you.'

She fell off her log with a screech of laughter that had clouds of parrots and hornbills rising in fright from the surrounding trees. She rolled on the ground for a full couple of minutes, a quaking, helpless quivering mountain of blubber and giggles. She sat up when she had recovered somewhat.

'Never mind about being too rough for me,' she chortled. 'I'll risk it. When you come back from your pygmies stay a couple of nights with me and we'll make good jumba [love] together.'

I smiled at her.

'Count on it, Lucy,' I lied. 'I wouldn't miss it for the world.'

I tried a couple of spoons of her stew. As I expected, it was monkey meat, a firm favourite of the forest African, if not entirely so of mine. The meat was dark and tough and stringy.

'I found him lying dead under a tree,' she explained, rather unnecessarily I thought. 'He must have been an old grandpappy, for he had a white beard, and he couldn't have been feeling very well for he was covered in boils.'

I was still chewing away unenthusiastically when I left her. I turned at the edge of the forest to wave back at her. She was still sitting on her log. Her teeth gleamed white in the gloom of the forest, and her fingers fluttered feebly at me in farewell salute, like the wings of the last butterfly of summer.

Once I was out of her sight I spat out the meat. Among the gristle was a large toenail, very much like an old man's toenail, ochre-yellow in colour, with a grainy appearance and curled over gruesomely at the end.

'How do you know it was a *monkey's* toenail?' asked Kamara with ghoulish relish when I told him about it.

To my delight, my first pygmy encampment was exactly as I imagined it would be, a circle of about thirty leafy, beehive-shaped huts in a clearing amidst enormous trees. It seemed deserted, but wisps of smoke from little cooking fires before the huts indicated that the inhabitants were not far away. I had heard that they were shy of strangers and I guessed that they were hiding in the surrounding undergrowth, watching to see whether we looked friendly. I had never smoked in my life but having been told that pygmies were complete slaves to the demon nicotine, I had come well stocked with cartons of cigarettes. I placed four packets on a tree stump nearby, sat down with my back against a tree, and waited.

I began to doze off in the dense, hot air. Suddenly, he was there before me. One moment, there was nothing but the somnolent churring of insects around me to suggest that anything lived here and the next, there he was. My first pygmy. He was quite the ugliest human being I had ever seen in my life.

He was standing on one leg before me, nervously, ready to vanish to whence he had come at the first sign of aggressive intent from me. He would have been, I reckoned, about sixty years of age, which would have made him, I was later to find out, very old by pygmy standards. He was coal black, barrel-chested, less than five feet in height, and with scrawny little Minnie-Mouse legs. He was stark naked, and he looked like a troll from one of the Brothers Grimm fairy tales of my childhood. His odour betrayed a chronic aversion to regular bathing habits.

He stabbed his chest with a bony forefinger. 'Me – Benjie!' he growled in a deep-brown Paul Robeson voice. He reached for a cigarette packet and removed a cigarette. He lit it with a brand from the fire at his feet. Then he cupped a hand to his mouth and uttered a loud halloo, a weird yodelling sound that reverberated throughout the treetops. Immediately, pygmies came drifting out of the surrounding bush in twos and threes, men, women and children. Although many were as black and unprepossessing as the one before me, some of the younger ones were very light-skinned, slender, and almost Pharaonic of mien. I wondered at the time if these could have been the result of miscegenation involving the African tribes from the villages skirting the forest, and I was to find out later that the latter did indeed enter into love affairs with pygmy girls on the odd occasion. (The pygmy girls, through generally completely faithful while married, could be quite flirtatious when single.)

These, then, were the people with whom I was due to live for the next few months. They would turn out to be quite the most entertaining months of my life.

Like all Africans who came from outwith these great forests, my porters were terrified of the little people. Highly exaggerated tales of their supposed lethal proclivities against those who earned their wrath circulated freely throughout the outside world, and their expertise with various virulent poisons extracted from the bark and leaves of the myriad plants growing around them was the stuff of campfire legend. They were taking no chances: they dumped their loads on the ground and insisted on an immediate return to Jacob's Camp. I paid them off and Kamara and I were left to our own devices. Kamara got a huge welcome from the pygmies, for he had been in this area before. It would take them some time to fully accept me, but accept me at last they did, and they seemed eventually to become quite proud of their 'white papa', as they began to call me. I, in turn, became equally proud to be accepted as one of them.

Kamara and I were each given a hut at the far end of the encampment. The huts were tiny, but snug and waterproof, composed of large green leaves lashed down with liane on to a framework of pliable saplings. I just about managed to get my whole body inside mine by curling myself up into a foetal position but there was no hope for Kamara's lanky six-foot-six frame. His legs sticking out through the tiny door afforded the pygmies much amusement. Luckily, it was the dry season so apart from offering his ankles on a nightly basis to a wide variety of bloodsucking insects, he did not suffer too much.

I was assigned a girl to look after my daily needs, such as lighting a fire for my morning tea, cooking for me, washing my clothes, and so on. Her name was Kumunbrusadé, but she was known to all and sundry as 'The Dancer', on account of her expertise in the art of dancing, a very important skill in the pygmy culture. I think she was about fifteen years of age, but it was really very difficult to tell, for pygmies matured early and, indeed, the girls generally married at puberty. The Dancer's husband had been killed the previous year by one of the mad little red forest buffaloes that abounded in the forest hereabouts. She was not altogether sorry that he had been killed, she told me, for he was a drunkard and he used to beat her badly when in his cups. Also, he snored horribly, and furthermore he was starting to get jealous of her dancing naked before the others at the pygmies' regular soirées, and how could a girl of her status be expected to properly express the freedom of 'The Dance' if she was being hampered by clothing? One night, she said, she would dance for me, and I would see for myself what she meant. This was now her 'Free Time' when, by pygmy law, she was allowed to have affairs with as many lovers as she wished until she next agreed to marry.

I was utterly enchanted by her. She was of a light caramel hue, slim and graceful of movement, and her only concession to clothing when we met was a small bunch of leaves hanging down her front from a vine tied around her waist. She only dressed like this while hidden away in the forest, she assured me; when going out to market, she put on her 'best clothes'. She showed me these – the sort of purple lace knickers one might have expected on an Armenian harlot, pathetic little scarlet shorts, and a white American T-shirt with, emblazoned on the chest in black lettering, the words 'Man Wanted' and on the back the words 'Apply Within'. Personally, I preferred her with just the bunch of leaves hanging down her front but she obviously thought that this rubbish was the very epitome of haute couture in the white man's world, and I could never have been so cruel as to try to disillusion her.

She was never still. She was always on the lookout for something to do for me, and her constant flirting somehow seemed so childlike and so innocent.

The pygmies had no tribal system such as the Africans outside the forest had, and thus they had no tribal chiefs. Benjie was the family head here, and therefore in charge of the encampment. Often of an evening he would invite me over to his hut to share his calabash of palm wine, that sweet, thick, floury extract from the wild palm so beloved of the people of the forest.

Sometime, he even accorded me the ultimate honour of asking me to dine with him. This could occasionally be a serious test of one's will to live, as on the occasion on which he asked me to a celebratory meal following the killing of a gorilla earlier that day. As I was a Guest of Honour, he said, the *pièce de résistance* would be mine. Amid much ceremonial beating of drums and tinkling of their 'bush xylophones', this was borne to me on a long green banana leaf. Boiled gorilla testicles. I gazed with revulsion at the wet, hairy mush before me, wondering how on earth I was going to be able to opt out of eating this disgusting mess without offending my host. I hit on an idea.

'This looks wonderful!' I exclaimed. 'But I must share it with Kamara in his hut, for he is my friend and we always share everything that we receive.'

With some reluctance, he allowed me to depart with my trophy. Inside Kamara's hut, an appalled Kamara gazed at the offering in dismay.

He stated firmly and quite unequivocably: 'Patron, I have had to try many a strange thing on the cattle trail, but thanks be to Allah the Great and the Good and the Merciful,

I have never had to put my lips on to the balls of a gorilla and long may that pleasant situation continue.'

He was industriously digging with the blade of his machete on the floor of his hut as he spoke. I tipped the soggy mess into the hole. He sang a dreary Fulani coronach as he covered up the mortal remains of one very large bull gorilla.

CHAPTER ELEVEN

The Great Okapi Dance

While I have always been pretty easy-going about what I eat to the extent that I have occasionally been accused of having a digestive system no more refined than that of the estuarine crocodile of Australasia, I have to admit that the staple pygmy diet came as something of a nasty surprise to me when I first encountered it. I had, in my naivety, assumed the pygmy to be an indefatigable hunter, one who hunted every day for the sheer joy of the hunt and lived on the almost exclusively carnivorous diet of antelope, guinea-fowl, wild pig, haunch of buffalo and the like, with the occasional comb of wild sweet honey thrown in for afters.

I was rapidly disillusioned. The male of the pygmy race, I soon discovered, hated work as a cat hates water. He was bone idle. The woman did the work, while the man did the sleeping and the loafing about. Man was the hunter, certainly, but he only went out hunting when driven to it by sheer necessity and the nagging tongues of his women.

So far as my pygmies were concerned, the necessity for hunting did not arise while they had a marsh full of tadpoles nearby. The tadpoles in the marsh were enormous things, a good four inches long with colossal globular heads and cute little smiles on their honest black faces. They were considered a delicacy by Benjie's mob. I did not consider them to be a delicacy at all but having elected to live as the pygmies did I felt that I could not, in all fairness, pick and choose how I lived my life with them, gorilla testicles perhaps excepted.

Every morning, therefore, until the tadpole season came to an end, the women would go down to a deep pool on the edge of the mere with buckets and all sorts of containers, fill them to the brim with swamp water and shoals of the squirming creatures, put them on the fire to boil, and hey presto! Polliwog Broth. It was not the sort of stuff you would order at a posh restaurant, for it was greyish black in colour, it was slimy, and it tasted of mud. It looked and smelt hellish, but it was as filling as porridge, which, I suppose, was all that mattered.

At the beginning of the dry season, the day of the first hunt drew near. The time considered most propitious, Benjie told me, was the time of the rising of the first full moon after the rains. As the time came ever closer, the air in the encampment seemed to crackle with anticipation. Now, even the men were so stirred from their torpor that they put some effort into preparing their weapons. Spear heads and arrow heads were sharpened to the keenness of cut-throat razors, old arrow hafts and spear shafts were replaced with fresh green ones cut from the forest and a variety of evil-looking poisons were concocted from vines and tree resins for doctoring their weapons. The women busied themselves repairing old nets and making new ones, and any child old enough to walk had a job to do, usually tending the cooking fires or carrying little calabashes of water on their heads from the nearest stream. Old Benjie, just wandered about, supervising the preparations. It was all hustle and bustle, a remarkable transformation from the usual somnolence exhibited by the denizens at other times.

At last, the big day dawned. On the afternoon before it, Benjie called me to his hut. Tonight, he told me, I would be his Guest of Honour at the traditional feast always held before a hunt to 'guide the hunters' arrows straight'. Tonight, he said, we would be joined by villagers from two other pygmy encampments, for the talking drums I had heard beating the previous night had invited them. Tonight, also, The Dancer would perform for us her 'Great Okapi Dance'.

The forests around us were rich in ground game. Most of this consisted of duiker, pangolin, ground squirrel, mongoose, bush pig, chevrotain, porcupine, and the like. I had heard that the elusive okapi ,while very scarce in this area, was occasionally caught in the pygmy hunting nets. They were the only creatures to escape the nets alive, said Benjie, for there was money in them. A white Frenchman, he said, came from Yaounde, the Cameroon capital, to Jacob's Camp at the time of each full moon to buy them. Benjie had no idea what the Frenchman did with them and cared less, although it as obvious to me that the animals were air-freighted to the zoos of Europe, where there was a lot more money to be made from their sale than Benjie would ever receive. Shy and secretive in the wild, the okapi adapted to captivity incredibly quickly, and became tame in no time at all. For a long time, this curious animal, always referred to as 'okapi' by the pygmies had been regarded as nothing more than a pygmy myth by sceptical scientists until one was captured at the beginning of the 20th century. About the size of a European roe deer, the okapi is in fact related to the giraffe. It has very giraffe-like horns, is of a dark-chocolate hue, with a white head and brilliant white lateral stripes on its rump and on the backs of its legs, a fly-switch tail and a narrow white patch highlighting its genital area. Like the giraffe, it packs quite a kick in its powerful back legs.

As it happened, I had already seen one, stone dead, shot by a white French hunter who was proudly exhibiting it to his friends in the forecourt of a meat-storage plant in far-off Yaounde where he had had it stored. God knows what he intended to do with the carcase; when he showed it to me he appeared simply to be wallowing in the glory of having shot an extremely rare trophy. It had been easier than he expected, he said. He had found its little one in the forest, and he had patiently waited until its bleating brought the mother out of the bush to suckle her baby. A shotgun filled with buckshot had solved the problem neatly insofar as the mother was concerned. The baby had died in the back of his truck on the way to the city, still trying to suckle its dead mother. There are still men like that around today, unfortunately, and not all of them reside beyond the shores of our own green and pleasant land, either.

Old Benjie hoped to net a few okapi on the morrow, because his pygmies, while clinging – albeit none too enthusi-astically – to the old ways, needed money to buy knick-knacks from the African market women outside the forest.

Meanwhile, he had tonight's party to organise, and it was a matter of pride for him that the party should be a good one. He had a couple of dozen calabashes of palm wine coming in from his favourite 'wine trees' in the forest, a dozen plump guinea-fowl ready for roasting, and a whole bushbuck smoking under leaves on a rack at the edge of an encampment. And The

Dancer, he informed me with a wicked little leer, had gone to her 'secret place' in the woods with some of the other women to get herself painted up for the dance, and to practise her choreography. The Okapi Dance, he promised, would be like no dance I had ever seen in my own country.

The moon was at its fullest. It was well into its long journey up the sky over the pygmy forests, and already it was bathing the clearing with its silvery light. High up in the tree canopy and far away from us the tree hyrax, cousin to the elephant but no bigger than a guinea pig, began its eerie rattling cry, a cry that rang out through the treetops above us, a cry that has been likened to that of a child being throttled. There was not a breath of wind, and the heavens sparkled with diamonds.

I sat on one side of Old Benjie, Kamara on the other. Kamara, being a strict Muslim, did not drink alcohol but Benjie and I were prepared to make up for his lack of good breeding. Our tin cups were filled to the brim and a flagon of palm wine sat on the ground between us. There was a trembling excitement in the hot humidity, and a low murmuring of expectation from the audience of pygmies thronged around the forest clearing. Musicians tinkled away prettily on their various instruments and gymnasts tumbled and somersaulted exuberantly before us. These I realised, were the warm-up acts for the Big Event of the evening.

The music stopped abruptly and the gymnasts capered off into the night. The crowd stopped their chatter and even the hyrax had ceased his chilling racket. An uncanny, brooding stillness had now descended over the forest.

It was a silence that was broken by a sharp tac-a-tac-a-tac... tac-a-tac-a-tac... tac-a-tac-a-tac from a solitary drummer, and The Dancer exploded into the arena in a whirlwind of arms and legs, her feet flickering in a veritable torrent of movement, movement so rapid that the eye could barely cope. She was completely naked. A pair of small horns was affixed to her brow, and her forehead, cheeks, ears and breasts were painted with white clay. Gleaming white lateral stripes adorned her bottom and the backs of her legs, while a scut of white wool protruding from the cleft of her buttocks completed her astonishing transformation to the world of the okapi.

She spun round and round on her toes like a ballerina, edging her way slowly but surely across the clearing until she was facing us. She paused momentarily, her body still except for her dancing feet, gazing at us with her doe-like eyes, smiling at us. Now a shudder ran through her whole body, from head to ankle. Her feet were now moving in prestissimo tempo. She reached out a hand and slowly stroked my forehead once, in a downward motion with the nail of her forefinger. Then she pulled at my earlobe, gently, twisting at it, chuckling wickedly. She did the same to Kamara, then she turned her back to us, flicked her scut cheekily at us, and was gone to the centre of the clearing in a glissading movement. Here she was joined by a similarly caparisoned, equally nude 'okapi' who had emerged like some ghostly emanation from the shadows. This one was a male, a well built, light-skinned youth whom I had never seen before and whom I guessed to be from one of the other pygmy villages. He was in a stage of extreme sexual excitement. The two embraced languorously, then danced off joyously across the clearing and into the surrounding trees, hand in hand together, to be replaced by the gymnasts and the musicians and the applause of the spectators.

It was the interval. Benjie handed me the flagon of palm wine.

'Let us drink, my friend,' he said. 'Soon The Dancer will be with us once more, back to perform her final dance; the Dance of the Okapi Hunt, and we don't want to miss that!'

She was back, in fact before we were more than half way through our next mug of palm wine. She was quite alone this time. One moment, the clearing was devoid of life and the next, she was there, standing in the middle of it, perfectly still, her slim form luminescent in the moonlight, poised like some heavenly gift to Mother Earth, her arms stretched upward towards the stars, an indescribably beautiful, golden-brown wraith in the act of laudation to her gods of the pygmy forests.

Four young men emerged from the darkness behind her. They wore loin cloths, and their faces were heavily streaked with the scarlet dye from the camwood tree, the traditional painting for pygmies going out on an important hunt. Between them they carried a large net

They stalked her in an exaggerated tiptoe fashion, lifting their feet high with each step, like secretary-birds stalking a venomous black cobra. She skipped away from them, lithe and silent as a woodland sprite. She stood facing them, arms uplifted again, a mocking little smile on her face, daring them, teasing them, urging them with gestures to try harder. Net outstretched, they moved in on her. Again she slid gracefully away from them. They moved across the arena in this way, the hunters stalking her with dramatised caution, she always managing to skip out of reach of her frustrated pursuers.

The thought had just crossed my mind that this was a scenario that could have gone on for ever when, by accident or design, they were upon her, wrapping her securely within the folds of the net, she bleating as okapis do when they are thus caught. The drums rolled in a triumphant Wagnerian crescendo of sound as the hunters disappeared with their net and their writhing captive into the gloom of the forest.

The Great Okapi Dance was over. I watched as pairs of young men and women from the spectators followed the hunters and their captive into the trees, followed them hand in hand into the trees, each man with his chosen girl until they too had disappeared from our sight and the clearing was empty of all living things apart from Old Benjie, Kamara, myself, and a few doddery elders whose days of hunting, dancing and lusting were well and truly behind them.

Tonight, I knew that the woods would resound to the sounds of jumba. Tonight, I knew that The Dancer would be dancing again, this time in some secret arbour among the ancient trees, dancing this time to a tune that was already old when her wonderful race of little people first arrived in the heart of this strange and incredibly beautiful continent, the land where Original Man had been conceived at the beginning of recorded time.

And, with him, Original Sin.

CHAPTER TWELVE

The Hunt

I was awakened just before dawn. Kamara was by my bedside, cup of tea to hand. The Dancer, he informed me, was recovering from her exertions of the night before, so he had taken over her duties.

The pre-dawn air had a chill to it. Women were boiling sweet wild yams they had dug up in the forest, to carry with them for their menfolk to the hunt. Their men, meanwhile, were sleepily engaged in getting their gear gathered together. The crossbow seemed to be a favourite with them. I examined one. It was a primitive contraption made from the wood of the dahoma tree, giving it both strength and flexibility. It was like a child's toy, so tiny was it compared to its English equivalent. The arrows were simple bamboo splints with iron points, while the spears were long, thin ebony saplings, a common enough plant in those dark wet forests around us. Each hunter carried a large roll of netting on his shoulders.

Today, our main target was the little duiker which had

the most prized meat of all forest antelopes. The women would be the 'beaters', driving the game to the nets. Each was armed with the traditional little pygmy machete for hacking their way through the tangles of thorny vines and for protection against snakes. Incongruously, each carried from a vine tied around her waist a couple of tin cans of the Heinz Baked Beans variety, obviously foraged from the villagers at Jacob's Camp, to clatter together in order to keep the game moving towards the nets.

The path was barely perceptible and the machetes came in handy. We were moving deeper and deeper into the forest, and the larger trees now consisted mainly of Triplochiton species, of the white 'obeche' timber so much in demand by the European plymills. The maple-like leaves of these gigantic trees made for a very loosely packed crown that let light filter down to the ground, allowing a dense vegetative cover to develop on the forest floor, ideal cover for the forest animals. It was also ideal cover for the creatures we wished to avoid.

Once, an irascible tree snake reared up around six feet away from my hat, to be despatched instantly by a machete, and I received a most painful sting on the ball of my thumb from a hairy green caterpillar lurking on the underside of a leaf I had carelessly grasped in passing. Tiny black buffalo flies swarmed around us in clouds, clogging the eyes, ears and nostrils, and a massive monitor lizard about five feet long, looking for all the world like a Komodo dragon, shot across the path hissing like a steam train and scaring the living daylights out of the lot of us.

This day, I had been told, would be divided into two drives. I decided to join the beaters for this one, for the women were in high spirits. Our track diverged from the men's path at a certain point, and we were now following a track even fainter than the one we had just left. The women began to sing, the high-pitched voice of Bilinga, the camp humorist, leading the others:

'Papa Don with we today, so hunting will be good,
Papa Don with we today, so hunting *must* be good,
White man juju very strong, so hunting must be good;
Animals, they fear white man,
So hunting *must* be good.
Animals all run to nets,
They run like hell, all to the nets,
For white man's juju strong, yah yah,
For white man's juju strong.'

When she had exhausted the humorous potential of this one,
she started on another one:

'Papa Don get power for bed,
So Papa Don will marry,
Marry little pygmy girl,
Papa Don will marry,
Papa Don will stay with we,
Stay with we for ever,
Papa Don with pygmy girl,
Stay with we for ever.'

We stopped here and there to gather mushrooms and the
big green fruit of the giant Makoré tree. The Makoré was only
ever an occasional tree in the rainforest, and it depended on the
elephant herds for its regeneration through their scattering of
its copious fruit harvest for miles around the parent tree. This
tree was vital to the pygmies, for the cooking oil extracted from
the seed kernel was of the purest quality. Unfortunately, as a
species it is, I fear, doomed, for it is as much sought-after as
mahogany.

By the end of our first drive, we had netted only one

blue duiker and three cane rats. The latter, about the size of Yorkshire terriers, were much prized as food throughout equatorial Africa. The nets were moved about a mile away for the afternoon drive. The nets, about three feet in width, were draped, section by section, over bushes and other vegetation until they had covered a length of about a couple of hundred yards. I stood by the end of one section, accompanied by a hunter named Cigarette, so-called because that was the only word of English at his command.

Almost instantly, Cigarette was involved in what could fairly be called the Drama of the Day. A huge aardvark blundered into our net. Cigarette, attempting to spear it, lost his footing and fell straight into the arms of the infuriated creature. The aardvark received him gladly, and made a valiant attempt to rip him apart. Fortunately, it was enmeshed in netting, so apart from slobbering copiously in Cigarette's face, not much damage was done. Cigarette was yelling his head off, and I was hopping around with his spear in my hand, unable to do anything very constructive with it for fear of transfixing Cigarette in the undignified imbroglio. Finally, the weird-looking monster solved the problem in its own way by ripping the net asunder and lumbering off into the forest with a garland of netting around its neck, emitting loud and sulphurous farts as it went, and leaving a badly shaken Cigarette behind, still wrapped up like a Christmas parcel in the remains of the net.

We headed for home at the end of the afternoon with nothing more to show for our day than the cane rats, the solitary duiker, and an evil-tempered Cigarette covered in bruises. Not one single okapi, and privately I was glad of it. Bilinga, inevitably, had some very scathing verses to sing on the way home about the inadequacy of a certain white man's juju and – to add fuel to Cigarette's already vile temper – a scurrilous song about a pygmy pervert whose idea of sexual gratification was being wrapped in a net in the arms of an aardvark.

🏚✕🏚✕🏚✕

It was, at last, time for me to leave. I was shivering a little in the now-familiar pre-dawn chill, ideal conditions for the start of our walk out of the forest.

All the pygmies were gathered round to see me off. To my joy, The Dancer was among them. I had seen very little of her during the past ten days, for I had been out with the hunters while she had remained behind in camp. She was smiling, but tears were running down her cheeks. She handed me a most beautiful purple orchid.

'I climbed the tall tree behind our camp yesterday to get this for you,' she whispered, 'to bless you with luck on your journey.'

Kamara appeared by her side. He looked strangely sheepish.

'Where is your gear, Kamara?' I queried. 'We have to go now.'

He hung his head.

'Sorry, Patron,' he mumbled. 'But I have decided to resign from your employ.'

I was staggered.

'Resign?' I spluttered. 'But I thought you were happy with me?'

'Yes, Patron, I have been very happy with you,' he assured me. 'But I shall be even happier with The Dancer. You see Patron,' he continued as I stood there, mouth open, staring at him, 'I am staying here. The Dancer and I are getting married.'

'Married?' I gawked. 'I didn't know …..'

111

He grinned at me.

'What do you think The Dancer and I were doing while you were away out in the bush fooling around on your daft hunts?'

I looked at him, momentarily speechless. I turned to The Dancer. She was sobbing unrestrainedly now. I put my arm around her. I recovered enough to do the decent thing and shake Kamara's hand, wishing him well. All around me were pygmy women and their toy children, all of them in tears. My carriers were waiting patiently. I knew that I had to get out of here, and right quickly at that.

The Dancer spoke in my ear.

'I hope you will never forget us,' she gulped.

I pushed her gently away from me, back into the arms of her future husband. I about turned and walked away from them, out through the silent throng of little people, not once looking back, not daring to look back, following my porters out of this incredible Shangri-la that had come to mean so much to me.

At times like these, sadness and happiness go hand in hand. You have just got to let go and keep walking before the whole thing gets on top of you.

CHAPTER THIRTEEN

Willi's Wahoo

His name was Willi Petrovitch.

He was Russian, and he claimed to have been one of the resident jesters in the Court of Rasputin when he was young. Most of us believed him, for his stories of the old Tsarist regime had an air of authenticity about them, and he would, I suppose, have belonged to the right timescale for it. He was, he said when I first met him in 1970, 93 years of age and, facially at least, he looked every bit of it. His face was as wrinkled as a prune, with a bushy grey moustache. But twinkling eyes betrayed a wicked sense of humour that was never far from the surface within him. He was tall and straight of back, too, with none of the usual body thickening of age, and he looked as fit as a flea. I was also soon to find that he harboured very young ideas under that snow-white thatch of his.

He lived in Douala, a seaport of quite extraordinary humidity and range of smells that had, over the centuries, arisen like a syphilitic chancre around the crotch of the

Bight of Benin. Although the area surrounding his place was a confused heterogeneity of mud huts and shacks of rusting corrugated iron, Willi lived in the relative opulence of one of the old French colonial compounds near to the Wouri River. His was a typical colonial building of solid breeze-block and massive iroko timbers. It even had its own electricity, supplied by an elderly Blackstone generator situated to the rear of the house. The compound was a blaze of colour throughout the dry season. Red-flowering hibiscus bushes were everywhere, and yellow-flowering cassias and scarlet flame-trees cast shade over the house during the heat of the day. Little bulbuls, waxbills and long-tailed whydahs twittered gaily among the seeding grasses and the pink harmattan lilies, while gorgeously hued sunbirds flickered in kaleidoscopic splendour around the purple bougainvillea climber that sprawled over his verandah.

All this was in pleasing contrast to the noisome squalor that surrounded his compound. The contents of open drains meandered with treacly sluggishness among the dwellings, their cargoes of human faeces bobbing their leisurely way down the rivers of urine to the Bight of Benin. Great hunchbacked rats roamed the alleyways in droves. Indeed, they were encouraged to take up residence here, Willi informed me, for the locals ate them. He himself had tried rat en brochette once upon a time at an African party. Not really to his taste, the old man admitted. A bit gamey, rather reminiscent of off-season grouse.

'Anyway,' he reflected with sublime Russian logic: 'One would expect rats that have spent their lives being marinated in the sewers and latrines of Douala to have a certain *je ne sais quoi* about the flesh by the time it is placed before one on the dinner table.'

The worst part about it all, he confided, was that the arôme lingered hauntingly on his taste buds, imparting an unforgettable flavour to his boiled egg at the breakfast table for weeks afterwards.

Willi had two main interests in life – women and fishing. The location of his quarters mean that he could indulge himself with those two hobbies whenever he chose to do so, for *Le Pecheur*, a rather snooty expatriate fishing club, lay five minutes' walk along the bank of the river to the south of his compound, while *Dani Bar*, a nightclub of singularly attractive girls of astonishing depravity lay a similar distance to the east of him along the alleyway between the shacks.

His welcome at *Dani Bar* always bordered on the rapturous, for Willi was rarely short of money. He was the local agent for a Russian shipping line, and this was a period when the Russians had begun to home in on the highly lucrative West African mahogany export trade in a big way.

There was less enthusiasm for his company at *Le Pecheur*, for the more hidebound of its members strongly disapproved of his sexual shenanigans. Indeed, a certain Club Night when the Russian had brought into the hallowed premises as his guest a young lady called Bébé from the nightclub would live long in their memory. Perhaps the young lady's mode of dress for this most formal of all Club functions did not help – scarlet leather boots that reached halfway up her shapely thighs, and an electric-blue skirt that barely covered her most precious commodity. In addition – horror of horrors – she was topless. The Lady President delegated to instruct her to cover up decently received a somewhat dusty reply for her pains: 'What's the matter, you ugly old vulture? Are you jealous of my tits?'

Old Willi's main claim to fame, however, did not rest entirely on his early relationship with the Court of Rasputin. Far more proud was he of the fact that he claimed the biggest wahoo in all of Africa. I first saw it in *Le Pecheur*.

Willi it was who introduced me to *Le Pecheur*. As expatriate clubs went in that day and age, there was, at first glance, nothing very special about this one. It was spotlessly clean, of course. The wooden flooring, bars, ceiling and furniture gleamed with constant polishing. A notice above the main bar proclaimed in Latin: *Bonum vinum laetificat cor hominus.* What set it apart from the others of its ilk was the fact that along the side wall was a glass case and it was a case that contained the clue to why a respectable Club like *Le Pecheur* would ever tolerate a reprobate like the old Russian on its premises. Inside the glass case, you see, was a large stuffed fish.

The fish was about five feet in length, very similar in shape and colouring to a barracuda. Willi stopped before it proudly.

'I believe it was a record for all of Africa when I caught it,' he informed me.

I looked at the inscription. *Willi's Wahoo*, the brass plate declared in beautiful copperplate script, *Acanthocybium solandari. Caught by Willi Petrovitch off Fernando Po Island on December 21st, 1952.*

'A memorable trip, in more ways than one,' mused the old man. 'I had gone over to Fernando Po with a French friend, and in a very short time I caught this wahoo. I had to get it back to the mainland rapidly before it deteriorated in the heat. Now, Fernando Po, though a tiny island, is covered with thick scrub, and many thousands of fruit bats roost there at night. My friend decided to stay on for a couple of days for some shooting among them.

'When he didn't return as scheduled, we sent a search party over. They returned rapidly, saying that he was still there all right, but raving mad and foaming at the mouth. Rabies from the bats. They were afraid to go near him. A posse of African gendarmes set sail, but returned a day later to say that he had vanished. Personally, I think that they shot him and dragged him down to the sea on the end of a piece of rope to feed the barracudas.'

He paused, then concluded: 'I don't blame them, but it put me off eating barracudas for a while.'

Willi left us suddenly during the night of his 95th birthday. He left us in style, too, by all accounts. After an evening of incredible vodka consumption at the nightclub, followed by a night of equally incredible bedroom activity for a man of his advanced years, his young partner Bébé woke to discover Willi lying stiff and cold in bed beside her. She left the compound at forty-five miles per hour, emitting the sort of sounds you would expect to hear from a highly-strung teenager who has just discovered the corpse of a nonagenarian lying in bed with her.

The old man died intestate and he left no provision for his burial costs. The members of *Le Pecheur*, never having been much interested in him while he was alive, were even less interested in him as a cadaver. In any case, the prize wahoo, their only link with him, was fast disintegrating, the white ants having at last begun to reduce it to powder. It was decided to take it down from the wall and chuck it into the sea.

Willi's body remained in the mortuary for quite some time, and it is possible that it might well have suffered the same fate as his wahoo had it not been for the generosity of the *Dani Bar* nightclub. The management purchased a grandiose mahogany coffin for him and paid for him to be given a decent

Christian burial at the exclusive expatriate cemetery up on the side of the Buea Mountain. Every single one of the harlots attended his funeral, probably the greatest gathering of whores ever seen in that quiet little town.

Evelyn, their matriarch, told me that in memory of old Willi, they had unanimously decided to give sex free of charge for the week following the funeral to the punters of *Dani Bar*. Also, she offered magnanimously, to the members of *Le Pecheur*, male and female.

'Mind you,' she added, 'most of them are already well known to us.'

Old Willi, I think, would have liked that final touch.

CHAPTER FOURTEEN

The Dancing Men

'**N**a Fir Chlis', the old people called them in the Gaelic of my childhood. The Dancing Men. To the more prosaic English-speaking world the phenomenon has always been known as the Northern Lights and the Aurora Borealis.

I had seen the Dancing Men more than a few times in the skies of my native Scotland, but never on the scale on which I was to see them over Canada's Lake Nipigon. Here when night descended they danced and swayed above the horizon in a graceful balletic movement of greens and reds and violets and never had the name given to them by my forefathers seemed more apt, for they resembled nothing so much as kilted dancers at a Scottish ceilidh enjoying a good old-fashioned knees-up.

I had been given the use of a rather battered old army jeep by a friend in Calgary, Alberta, and I was making good use of it. I had time to spare, so I had decided on a sight-seeing trip across Canada doing a bit of fishing en route, being as self-sufficient as possible. With this aim in mind, I had a couple of fishing rods and a single-barrelled 12-gauge shotgun in the back of my jeep, the latter being for duck and jack-rabbits to vary my diet as much as possible. Thus it was that I found myself in a general store in the town of Thunder Bay at the head of Lake Superior, talking to the proprietor.

'If you're lookin' for a really quiet place to fish,' he advised, 'you cain't do much better than try the Lake Nipigon area. It's only about forty miles to the north of here. I can even introduce you to a good guide for the area. Cherokee Joe. He knows the place like the back of his hand and he won't be too expensive.'

He paused while I paid for my purchases, then he continued, 'He's here in town and I think I know where to find him'.

As he was locking up, he turned to me.

'One word of warning, though: don't pay him a cent until the trip is over or he's liable to disappear on you.'

'Disappear?'

'Yep. Disappear. He's a bugger for the women and he cain't keep away from them. There are no women around the Nipigon area. At least, not Cherokee Joe's kind. Too remote. You are liable to waken one morning and find that he has high-tailed it back to town when he gets horny. Don't pay him until you've completely finished with him. As long as you're owing him money, he won't leave you.'

We located Cherokee Joe in the busiest bar in town. He was obviously Indian; tall, whipcord-lean and very good looking, something like a brown-skinned Randolph Scott, and he was surrounded by nubile young ladies in various stages of deshabille. He was also tipsy, but not so tipsy that he was unable to drive a hard bargain over his fee. He had an old Ford pickup truck, he said, and I could follow him in my jeep to the Nipigon area the following morning. He tried to cadge an advance from me, but remembering the storekeeper's advice, I refused. We parted on good terms, though, and I was just happy to have found someone who could show me around.

We set up camp by Lake Nipigon. He chose to sleep in his truck, while I erected by tent nearby. I was curious at the fact that absolutely all of the floor space in the back of his truck was taken up by a magnificent new spring mattress.

'You obviously like your home comforts, Joe,' I remarked.

He winked.

'You gotta be prepared,' he smiled enigmatically. 'A man never knows his luck.'

I got my rod out to test the water. With the ice just off the land, the fish were in a veritable feeding frenzy. One after another, I hooked and discarded a dozen or so little trout, none of them more than eight inches long. But I was content. The day was one of those beautiful Canadian days you often get at the very beginning of spring, all blue skies and gentle zephyrs and fragrances from all things growing. Cherokee Joe was also content. He was lying in the shade of some aspens a little distance up the hill behind me, sucking at a bottle of bourbon he had smuggled in from town.

My lure was taken viciously. A large lake trout, in the fifteen pound region, I would have guessed. It headed immediately for a sprawling willow bush whose branches trailed over the water surface. Here, it became hopelessly entangled. I frantically besought the help of my guide, only to be ignored by him.

The ensuring conversation went something like this:

'Joe, put down that bloody bottle and come here and help me.'

'Sod off!'

'You lazy Injun bastard, get your brown ass over here or I'll break that bloody bottle over your thick head.'

'Piss off, you ugly white monkey.'

He began to sing then, raucously, drunkenly, the first verse of a long and extremely vulgar song. A fierce lunge from the trout separated it from the hook. It vanished into the dark depths, while the silver spoon dangled forlornly from the willow tendril. I sighed, put down my rod, and began to wade out to retrieve my lure.

✦✦✦✦✦✦

I learned from that incident that it was wise to keep Joe away from the liquor during the day. Sober, he was the nicest guy you could ever wish to meet. Drunk, he was a downright liability. However, once we had certain ground rules established, we became good friends.

The area was a wildlife paradise. Moose flitted around the lake verges like lugubrious escapees from the dawn of time. Joe showed me a beaver dam about a mile from our camp. As we approached, an otter plunged into the water behind it. Otter, Joe informed me, had been known to bore holes in beaver dams so that when the water drained away, the fish were left high and dry for them to catch at their leisure.

The beautiful blue martin had already arrived from its winter holidays in South America, and its melodic rolling twitter filled the air above us. Kiskadees zigzagged about us, mouths agape as they flew in and out of the small swarms of insects, and the bubbling call of the mocking bird in the tall birch behind our camp made our days a complete joy.

From my childhood days of fishing with fly in the wee burns of Scotland, I have always harboured a special affection for this simple type of angling. During my visits to Canada, I developed a special affection for brook trout. I soon found that the feeder streams around us were full of them.

Brook trout are common in many parts of southern and eastern Canada. They are the most beautiful of fish. Scientifically dubbed as being one of the great family of char, they are, in my humble opinion, even better than arctic char in every way, the numerous spots on their bodies showing up a vivid red against a sleek olive-brown background. The broad streak of crimson running from head to tail along the lower flank completes a picture that is little short of perfection.

And 'perfection' is certainly what you will think when you have it on the plate before you for the first time. Anyone who has ever eaten a brookie will never look at salmon in the same light again. If there is a tastier fish in the whole wide world, I have yet to find it.

The brook trout is an angler's dream. They take bait and lures avidly and provide a hard and exciting fight. Here in the Nipigon area they averaged less than a pound in weight, but even at this weight they were doughty fighters, and Joe told me that further into the interior weights of over six pounds were not unheard of.

The aura of peace around this beautiful place was such that I could have stayed here until time was with me no more. Perhaps predictably my contentment was disrupted, rudely and finally, by Cherokee Joe and his penchant for the pleasures of Bacchus.

Joe had borrowed my shotgun to go off upstream to look for duck. I stayed around our campsite, repairing fishing tackle and gathering firewood. I was returning from the woods with a bundle of sticks under my arm when a cab pulled up beside me. A Thunder Bay address on the side of the vehicle, I was quick to note. The door opened, and out stepped quite the most extraordinary vision I had ever seen within a hundred miles of any fishing camp.

Her face was a face surely crafted by angels to tempt the Devil, and her perfect breasts were covered – if that's the word I want – with the merest morsel of transparent silk. Her impossibly long, impossibly lovely legs were crowned by the briefest mini-skirt you ever did see and her flaxen hair swept down to her waist. Her toenails were of a deep maroon hue, her fingernails primrose yellow. Her legs were a flawless golden brown in colour. She was knickerless, a fact proven almost immediately by a sudden treacherous gust of wind. She made no attempt to cover her modesty. Her gorgeous smile simply broadened and she held out her hand to me.

'Hi!' she said in a throaty Brigitte Bardot voice. 'I'm Helga. I'm a friend of Cherokee Joe. He asked me to try to meet him here to keep him from feeling too lonely.'

Her accent was quite pronounced and I guessed it to be Scandinavian.

She continued: 'Can you pay the cabbie, please? It's fifty dollars, and I'm short of money. Joe will pay you back.'

I suspected that Cherokee Joe would do no such thing, but I paid the cabbie, albeit reluctantly, then shook hands with her.

'I do apologise,' I said somewhat dryly. 'If I had known you were coming, I've had the champagne chilled. Where are you from?'

'I work in a bar in Thunder Bay,' she said, 'but I'm from Finland. I met Cherokee Joe in town the night before he came out here with you.'

She took a long gold cigarette-holder from her bag and stuck a black Sobranie into it. 'He told me you had hired him for a trip out here.'

She paused while she lit up.

'Your name is Don, and you're a Scat huh?'

She rolled a little puff of smoke over my head slowly and sensually.

I was stricken dumb. This bloody woman is a sexual bombshell, I thought desperately. What the hell did Cherokee Joe think he was doing, inviting a damned bargirl out to a place like this? Couldn't he have tied a knot in it or something until he got back to town? I stood before her now, hand on chin, gazing at her, trying to figure out what on earth to do with her.

She spoke again, her accent thickening now, like treacle oozing from an oaken barrel.

'Joe ees *so* kind. He says he weel teach me how to feesh, and he weel teach me all about Nature in ze Raw out here in ze wilds.'

Her gorgeous eyes were sparkling with mischief and her smile would have created havoc with the Father, the Son and the Holy Ghost combined. Not to mention all the bloody Disciples, too, I thought with considerable feeling. She took a long, slow draw from her cigarette-holder, her eyes fixed on mine, challengingly.

'Weel *you* help heem teach me about Nature in ze Raw out here, Don?'

I drew a deep breath and tried to control my fast disintegrating senses.

'Trust me, Helga,' I replied, 'Cherokee Joe doesn't need

anyone to help him teach you about Nature in the Raw. Nature doesn't come any rawer than Cherokee Joe himself, and by all accounts he's a right good teacher.'

Her smile was enigmatic now.

'Well, we might as well make the best of it until he gets back. Sorry I don't have any of your Scottish whisky, so we'll have to share this Finnish stuff.'

She delved into her bag and produced a bottle of vodka.

I gave up.

'Let's sit down by the waterside,' I said. 'I have never drunk Finnish vodka before and drinking it with a good-looking Finnish lady seems as good a way to start as any.'

We had made serious inroads into the vodka by the time Cherokee Joe returned. He did not seem in the least surprised to see Helga. Their reunion was exuberant. They ate little, drank a lot, and went to bed early. I sat by the little fire as the evening shadows crept over the lake until, quite suddenly, night was upon us. I threw another couple of sticks on the fire to keep it going and retired to my tent.

I was soon to discover that it was not to be a night devoid of sound. Far off in the dark woods a family of timber wolves began to yowl plaintively, to be answered at once by the sharp squall of a coyote somewhere out there beyond the treeline. Behind my tent a screech owl uttered that most chilling of all owl calls, and from somewhere up the hill the repetitive booming hoot of the great horned owl was guaranteed to keep one's heart leaping convulsively and painfully in its frame. In the rushes by the lake about two million bullfrogs had started orchestrating with their curious and penetrating bellowing grunts. The human race, not to be outdone, had got into the act, too. From the truck beside my tent, Cherokee tribal whoops mingled discordantly with bouts of Finnish yodelling, while rhythmic squeaking sounds indicated that something in the truck badly needed oiling.

Sleep was impossible. All it needed now, I thought bitterly, was for the Great God Pan to march around my tent all night long playing his bloody pipes. I got up and walked down to the side of the lake. The skies were clear, and there was a touch of frost. As if on cue, the frogs ceased their uproar. Not so, alas, the lovers. They were giving tongue lustily in a staccato arpeggio tempo, and the truck was shaking like a cottonwood tree being buffeted by a sub-polar gale.

I gazed out over the lake towards the northern skies. All along the horizon the Dancing Men merged and separated, merged and separated, rolled and roistered about the firmament, in an erotic, humping extravaganza of movement and colour. One of them, I could almost have sworn, cocked his head and winked lasciviously down at me. I walked back to my tent. The frogs had resumed their racket and the trumpeting from within the truck had reached new heights of musical anarchy.

I looked at my watch. It was not yet midnight. Already, I could sense that I was in for a long, long night.

CHAPTER FIFTEEN

Screech on the Rock

Modern geographers call it Newfoundland, but it has been called many things in its time, most of them uncomplimentary. Even today's natives call it the Rock, and God knows what the original inhabitants called it. Today's inhabitants, you will almost certainly feel on first sighting it, have got it about right. Especially when you are at the end of a very long and tiring flight over the broad Atlantic and you are seeing it for the first time.

You see below you this great lump of wet black rock sticking up out of the sea and you wonder, firstly, how any human being could possibly live there and secondly, what the hell made you contemplate coming here in the first place.

The few colours you see are so funereal: the sombre loden hue of stunted spruces and jack pines trying to eke a living from the thin layer of acid soil that covers so much of the island; the forbidding cinereal masses of parent rock on which, surely, nothing at all but lichens could possibly survive; the patches and squiggles and ribbons of leaden water that are as much a part of this strange land as are the trees and the boulders and the rain.

The glaciers of the Pleistocene epoch determined the structure of the Newfoundland of today. They scraped off most of the topsoil from the parent rock, helping create the deep, fertile soils of the Canadian prairies to the west while in their slow, grinding march eastward, the glaciers dumped the soil and the nutrients that were to form the basis of the world-renowned Grand Bank fishing grounds – ironically, to be for so long a vital part of the economy of the island.

The original inhabitants were the Beothucks. They lived almost entirely by fishing, and they were the most peaceful of races. They were also reckoned to be the tallest of the North American Indian tribes, heights of six feet and slightly over being not uncommon among them. (Interestingly, the term 'Red Indian' would appear to have originated from the Beothuck habit of daubing their bodies with red dye for ceremonial purposes.) But influxes of Micmac Indians from mainland Canada combined with intrusions of piratical Basque, English and French seamen finished them off. Today, their race is extinct.

The ubiquitous Norsemen were here, too, at L'anse-aux-meadows on the northern-most tip of the island, a thousand years ago. They hung around long enough to build a few strong sod-and-wood structures, a forge for smelting iron, and some workshops. Then, having left for posterity this proof of their having been here, they vanished for ever into the Atlantic mists.

The current generation of islanders are, to a great extent, descended from people who came over the sea from Devon, Cornwall, Somerset and Catholic Ireland around the end of the 19th century, hoping to start a new and better life for themselves away from the privations of their own lands. Their first winter on the Rock must have made them wonder what they had let themselves in for.

Tourist literature understandably emphasises that Newfoundland summers are usually warm and pleasant, while under-emphasising the fact that winters can be very harsh indeed. I lived there for three years and my main memories of winter are of snow and ice and fog and freezing rain, the latter a phenomenon I had never experienced before. Rain falls from above as ordinary rain, but it freezes solid the moment it touches anything. It makes driving a particular hazard, with windscreen wipers quite unable to cope. A walk along the supremely draughty Water Street in the capital city of St John's with the wind blowing straight in from the Arctic icefields is enough to have the Virgin Mary dream unholy dreams of cosy pub fires and jugs of steaming punch.

A proud boast of the island's tourist board is that there are no skunks, snakes or ragweed on Newfoundland. They are also justifiably proud of the friendliness of their people and their unstinted generosity to strangers. This is particularly evident when one visits the outports, the tiny fishing communities clinging so precariously to the bare cliffs and rocks of the coastline.

A winter night in one of those rambling wooden shacks, being entertained by an old 'skipper' and his myriad relatives, is one for the scrapbook, that it is to say if all signs of life in your body have not been declared extinguished by the following morning. When the fiddles and the melodeons and the jew's harps get going and the drink is flowing as though tomorrow will never come, it is time for weaklings to dive for cover. Especially among the 'Irish communities'. None of those I met in the outports had ever been to Ireland, mainly, I suppose, because thousands of empty and often turbulent seas separate the Emerald Isle and the Rock, but close your eyes and minds for a moment or two during their ceilidhs and listen. Just listen, and you could be back among the bogs and the curlews of Cork and Kerry and Galway. The brogue is the same, rich and melodious and with the tang of peat and myrtle and new-mown hay about it, and the music could only be of Celtic origin, even if the lyrics of their songs are so very decidedly Newfoundland. You never feel too far from the land of their forebears when you are whooping it up among the fishermen of the Rock.

Things change, of course, and they are still changing even as I write. As surely as the Beothucks and the Vikings vanished, so too will the old ways and the dialects disappear with the going of the old folks. The young will become more and more Canadian in every way. It is inevitable. It has, after all, been thirty years since I was last in Newfoundland. If some of what I have written so far has been in the present tense, I try to excuse myself by saying that it seems like only yesterday since I was on the Rock myself.

Like many of my generation, I suffer from an incurable ailment. It is called chronic nostalgia, and I clutch at the past with the desperation of one who realises that both the past and the present are fast slipping away from him. In vain, I try to ignore the sad words of that perennial cynic Dorothy Parker: '....for tomorrow never comes, but alas it always does....' Yesterday will always be my tomorrow, and I cling, despairingly and unrealistically, to a past that can never return. Right now, I cling to the hope that even in this computer era of dot.com.

slash gibberish there might still be places in Newfoundland's outports where the squeezebox and the fiddle can still be heard, and the Oul' Fellas are still singing songs about Squid Jigging Grounds and Little Grey Hens as they did back when the world was young and I was younger.

And the drink. Let's not forget the drink, for the luvva Jasus. A hooley in a Newfie outport would be like a wake without a healthy-looking corpse if a man didn't have a jar or two to loobericate de oul' tonsils. And what better looberication could you find than Newfoundland's very own drink, the aptly named 'Screech'?

Screech has been described as a 'kind of rum' by someone who had obviously never sampled the stuff in his life. 'A kind of rum', forsooth! Such a bland classification does not even come close to describing Screech. I doubt, mind you, whether anyone could adequately describe it, especially the Screech made in the old days before it was legalised by the Government. Old Newfoundlanders regarded it as a cure-all, and I am at one with them in that. In its original form, that stuff would have cured anthrax. But describing it as a 'kind of rum' is like saying that King Herod was a social worker or that Hitler was a kind of house painter. Screech, it its original form, was alcohol of the basest kind.

'The best stuff,' one old timer assured me, 'was the stuff we made in the old days, before the Government took it over and made it fit only for namby-pambies. Black as a witch's tit, and it would have stripped the hair from your fundamentals.' All sorts of liver-improving agencies such as pure lemon extract, horse molasses, spit, chewing tobacco and wood alcohol were added to what had been, when initially smuggled into Newfoundland as the lowest possible grade of rum, a lethal enough hooch on its own.

The rum was smuggled in by the barrel from the French islands of St Pierre et Miquelon, just off the southern tip of Newfoundland's Burin Peninsula, usually at dead of night to avoid the customs cutters and the gunboats of the Royal Canadian Mounted Police. The Mounties in particular were much feared, as they tended to exhibit a most unhealthy curiosity when confronted by barrel-laden skiffs slipping silently through the waves at dead o' night, and their robust handling of those who broke the law had made their name a byword for obduracy among all God-fearing Newfoundlanders.

The skiffs used by the smugglers were not always in the first flush of youth and the risks taken were enormous. The seas running through the narrow channel between the French islands and the Newfoundland coast were treacherous, so dangerously overloaded vessels were in constant peril. Even in the most favourable conditions, barrels would often be lost overboard.

It was, therefore, not unknown for fishermen out innocently checking their lobster traps to happen upon a floating barrel. While every effort would of course be made to contact the Mounties about such finds – for the outport fisherman of Newfoundland would no more think of defrauding the Customs and Excise than the next person – it is a well known fact that you can never find a policeman when you want one. A major worry was that floating barrels could be a terrible hazard to high-speed patrol boats, and no law-abiding citizen would have wanted the loss of a police vessel on his conscience.

So, one did one's duty and lashed a rope – always kept handy in the boat against just such an emergency – to the cask and towed it ashore. A colossal Mountie, investigating one such incident at the college in which I worked remarked rather bitterly to me: 'Scottie, I'm due to retire soon, and the day that one of these bloody fishermen report finding one of these barrels to me, well, I shall regard it as the highlight of my career.'

One old 'skipper' – whom I shall call 'Patsy', for reasons that may become clear as the story unfolds – told me of the time he came upon one such barrel bobbing about in the sea when he was out in his little rowing boat. Patsy was a practical man, and he had few scruples about putting one over authority. Unlike the average outport fisherman, Patsy was a greedy man. He had a large and thirsty family, and he knew that he and his family were perfectly capable of taking care of the contents of the barrel without any assistance from his equally thirsty neighbours in the village in which he lived. He pondered the matter carefully, then he decided that the sensible thing to do would be to tow the barrel into the lee of the cliffs below his village, moor it there out of sight, then return for it after dark with his family when none other could observe them with their prize.

It was a long and excruciatingly stiff haul up the cliff track to the village, and there was much muted cursing at shins, knees and knuckles being barked as the family levered and shoved the laden barrel inch by painful inch upward. It was a pitch dark night, and the path being little more than a goat track, was narrow and wet and slippery. On more than one occasion only the lovely sloshing sounds from within the barrel and the thought of how good its contents would taste when they eventually reached home, kept them from abandoning the whole project. But, eventually, they made it.

It was near dawn when they finally set the barrel upright on their kitchen floor. Utterly exhausted, they sat around the barrel bereft of speech, prolonging with the sweet agony of anticipation that glorious moment when they would savour the heavenly nectar within. Finally, old Patsy stood up.

'Get your mugs ready, boys,' he said. 'We're going to

enjoy this!'

He levered the bung from the barrel and inhaled slowly, luxuriantly ......

This is not a tale with a happy ending and a short explanation is necessary hereabouts before we get down to the great denouement. In the Newfoundland of the 1960s, outport toilets were not the most modern in the world. Often the fish-gutting shed at the end of the long gangway jutting out to sea had to double as a toilet shed, with the human effluent joining the fish gurry to feed the marine life below. Where dwellings were some distance inland however, the traditional outdoor privy complete with bucket became the norm. It was Patsy's bad luck that one household somewhere further up the coast had hit upon the novel idea to save themselves the daily trek to the ocean with their bucket of ordure. A redundant rum barrel had seemed to them to be just the ticket. It would take weeks to fill, they reasoned, and once filled to capacity, all that remained to be done was to hammer in the bung, roll the thing over the fields to the edge of the cliff, and consign it to the deep .....

In the end, the Government of Newfoundland and Labrador found that they were making little impact upon the illicit trade in Screech. They did the sensible thing – they muscled in on it themselves. They legalised it, imposed the usual taxes, and now it is sold in liquor stores throughout the Province, the bottles most fetchingly labelled and proudly bearing the banner: *Famous Newfoundland Screech*. It is a big hit with tourists. It cannot hope to be as good as the real McCoy, of course, lacking as it does vital ingredients such as well-chewed tobacco. But it is still a pretty potent beverage.

Once upon a time I took a bottle of Screech home to my father in Scotland. The Old Man – an enthusiastic drinker of all that was best in Scotch whisky – was convinced that I was trying to kill him. He finished the bottle just the same, mind you, for the Old Man was ever willing to experiment in alcohol in the interest of research, but he maintained ever afterwards that the outport seamen of Newfoundland must have been equipped with the digestive tracts of saltwater crocodiles.

The Old Man didn't know the half of it. A long and rough night on the Screech followed by the traditional Newfie breakfast of 'fish and brewis' – a porridge of ship's biscuits and salt cod boiled to a pulp with a panful of piping-hot pork fat poured over the resultant mush – would have signed the death warrant of all but the hardiest of crocodiles, saltwater or otherwise.

'Let's bugger off up-country for a week or two and do a bit of fishing,' suggested Malcolm McDonald one summer evening as we sat in his house paying homage to the grand old Scottish pastime of emptying a bottle of Teacher's finest. 'It'll give you a memory of the Rock to carry away with you.'

The year was 1970. I had been three years in Newfoundland and I would be leaving the Rock in the autumn, returning to the rainforests of tropical Africa. I had no particular reason for leaving the island, for I had fallen in love with it. I loved the people and my work; indeed I loved everything about this primitive, incredibly beautiful part of Canada and I knew that I was going to hate leaving here more than I had ever hated leaving anywhere else. But, to employ a dreadful cliché, those who are born under a wandering star have little choice in the matter. To the insatiable wanderer, three years is a long time to live in any one place, no matter how great is your affection for that place. When the bug starts to bite, you have to move on.

The call of Africa had returned, ever more strongly and ever more insistently with the passage of each day, and I knew that I had to leave. Come the first chill wind of the late autumn I would be gone like the migrant robin off to warmer climes. I was aware, of course, that the Africa I had known in my youth was no more, that a widespread tribal unrest had made it a much less pleasant place to work in than of yore. But I had no qualms, for the true wanderer has no regrets, and he never worries about what may lie ahead of him. However uncertain the prospect before him, each new situation is a new experience, a new adventure leaving the past as mere phantasmagoria to be retained in a secret part of his mind as insurance against the boredom of old age, golden memories to sift through at leisure when the body no longer has the ability to respond to the call of the open highway.

Malcolm had purchased a new luxury Range Rover, complete with cooking and sleeping facilities within. He could, he reckoned, easily arrange time off work. He was a partner in a large medical practice in St John's – and, as his great passions were angling and the study of wildlife, he had decided that this would be as good a way of combining the two as any while, at the same time, testing his new vehicle in rugged conditions. He had had a rack installed on the roof of the vehicle to carry a 20-foot long canoe to give us access to the lakes of the interior.

'I'm all for it,' I responded. 'When shall we do it?'

'We'll take off as soon as I get the work situation sorted out,' he said. 'We'll get in the Land Rover, keep driving north, and stop wherever we want and for as long as we like. Whichever place takes our fancy, that's where we'll camp for the night.'

It was to prove to be the best holiday I would ever have in my life. From its southern-most point to its most northerly tip, Newfoundland is well over 700 miles long and most of that mileage is through pretty rugged territory. We were to cover a large part of that 700 miles by the time our trip came to an end. Malcolm had a prearrangement to pick up a teaching friend of his at Deer Lake, 400 miles off the beaten track on the other side of the island, but apart from that diversion, we had no plans made. We would just drift along and take it day by day. This was to be a trip devoted to such hedonistic pleasures as doing exactly what we liked, exploring parts of Newfoundland unfamiliar to us, communing with nature, and fishing. Most certainly, fishing.

The weather was superb, and the scenery out of this world. We fished and camped in places with marvellously evocative names, names like 'Rattling Brook', 'Leading Tickles' and 'Thunder Lake', and as it was still early summer and the fish were ravenous from their long winter fast, they took freely. At that time of the year it seemed to me that virtually every puddle of water in Newfoundland contained trout of a size and quality unknown back in my own country.

Often though, we did not even bother to fish, but would stop at some quiet spot to admire the glorious coastal scenery and to look at the wildlife. Auks, murres, guillemots and kitti-wakes were in abundance around the shores, and once we saw a couple of black bears on a fire-ravaged slope trying to uproot a charred stump in an endeavour to winkle out from under it something or other that had attracted their attention.

Signs of beaver and muskrat were evident in a number of places, hares lolloped ahead of us through the sparse scrub, and a huge, lugubrious moose watched us, bug-eyed, at the far end of a shallow muskeg, great strings of green water-weeds dangling from its antlers.

Nights were magical. We would pull in at some suitably lonely spot, always beside fresh water, for this was necessary for cooking and bathing and – most importantly of all – for our early morning tea. We tried to ensure that we were installed in our camping site in time to catch a trout or two for our evening meal, and our catch would be in the pan by dusk, by which time the birds would have gathered in the willows by the creek to express satisfaction with their own day.

Often, when darkness had fallen and the usual camping chores had been taken care of, we would sit by the fire exchanging yarns. Just as often, though, we would sit silent, drams in hand, watching the great Canadian moon edging its way slowly over the dark horizon, marvelling at the majesty of that amazing starlit sky. Real friends rarely require the crutch of chatter to bolster their friendship and in any case, when the gentle zephyrs of a Newfoundland night are sighing through the fir needles with the music of Aeolian harps, who needs the discordant sound of human voices?

Sometimes we fished from the canoe on the lakes (or 'ponds' as the smaller lakes are known in Newfoundland) and sometimes a stream or small river would take our fancy and we would fish from the bank.

We even put out to sea, and the cod took as freely as their freshwater cousins had been doing. And to those readers whose only contact with cod has been that purchased from some fish-and-chip shop and coated in thick greasy batter, take it from one who knows that the latter is a fraud. A fish from the sea, once frozen, never tastes quite the same, and the longer it stays frozen, the less it begins to taste like anything much, never mind fish. When the tang of the sea is still on your cod as you place it on the pan, and the waves are lapping gently against the shore a few yards away, and the sticks on your cooking fire are throwing showers of golden sparks upward into the Canadian night, and the little resin bubbles on the bark are popping in the heat to release delicate fragrances of turpentine and balsam and Mother Nature's unique, mysterious perfume, and the wild, lonely cry of some night bird is echoing out over the rippling waters before you, then you know – you just *know* – that you are as close to Paradise as you are likely to be on this earth.

We headed up the Northern Peninsula towards the town of Roddickton. It was here that we were due to meet one of Newfoundland's most respected sons. Earl Pilgrim had been a renowned boxer in the recent past and I had got to know him very well indeed in the city of St John's when he and a dozen of his forestry colleagues had been undergoing an extended course for Senior Forest Rangers under my guidance. At the time of our visit Earl was in charge of the forestry and wildlife department for the northern part of the island. Earl was a big chap with the body of a Greek god and with looks so good that no one meeting him for the first time would have imagined that he could ever have been mixed up in the brutal world of the prize-fighter, let alone having been very successful at it.

Earl was at home. I introduced him to the others and explained that, as our trip was nearing an end, we wanted a couple of days productive fishing to fill the two large cooler-boxes we had brought with us for the benefit of the folks back in St John's. He directed us to Cole's Pond, a lake well away from the beaten track. We fished there, and how inadequate the statement 'we fished there' looks as I write it. It was fishing all right, but what fishing! I have never known fishing like it, before or since.

We caught many fine specimens – brown trout, rainbows, Arctic char – and we released many back to the water to fight another day. By the end of our allotted time we had filled our coolers with the very best of our catch, and by the end of each day the crisp air and the sun and the salt breezes from the ocean beyond the Peninsula had given us an appetite that cannot be acquired in any city. We packed the coolers with ice to preserve the fish and drove off down that dusty track, away from Roddickton, away from Cole's Pond, away from that lovely, lonely wilderness, none of us showing any inclination for conversation and none of us daring to look back.

I have never held a rod in my hand since that day, and I have never had any wish to do so.

Newfoundland. 'A monstrous mass of rock and gravel ... a strange thing from the bottom of the deep ...' some philistine once wrote.

I beg to differ. I have found nothing but beauty in Newfoundland, beauty in her forests, beauty in her bogs, beauty in her barrens. Above all, I have found nothing but beauty among her hardy, enduring inhabitants.

I had much fun with the people of Newfoundland. Some of the best nights I have ever had in my life were among the fishing families of the outports. Time changes things, of course, and not always for the better. Once upon a time the Grand Banks were famed world-wide for their seemingly unlimited stock of fish. The seas around Newfoundland teemed with cod, to the extent that it is claimed that in the latter part of the nineteenth century one had only to lower a tin bathtub into the sea and it would come up full of cod. To the Newfoundlander, the names 'cod' and 'fish' were synonymous.

The outport fisherman never made a lot of money out of his fishing and it was a hard and dangerous way to make a living. But it *was* a livelihood, his way of life and he was fiercely proud of the fact that he was a fisherman.

Today, all that has gone. High-tech trawling combined with very modern greed has seen the piranhas of all the big fishing nations of the world descending on the Grand Banks in a feeding frenzy the like of which had never been known anywhere before. It may very well get worse too, for the great white sharks of the oil industry are reported to be cruising round the area, and they have rarely been noted for improving the environment or the lot of the little people.

Some years ago I received a surprise package from the then-Minister of Fisheries for Newfoundland and Labrador. Among its contents was a small Newfoundland pennant. It stands on my desk as I write this. Beside it stands a miniature bottle of Newfoundland's Famous Screech, still unopened, sent to me by a young Newfoundland friend, Janet McDonald, the daughter of my friend Malcolm.

As I gaze at those two little items, there is an almost tangible aura of deep poignancy in the room and a deep sadness within me that I fear will always be with me, for my dear friend Malcolm is no longer with us and if ever we fish together again it will be in some heavenly glade where all good fishermen go when their time on earth is over. But I am sure that, excellent though the fishing Up There must undoubtedly be, it cannot possibly be half as good as that which we experienced together on that long ago summer on the beautiful Rock.

As my eyes linger on that pennant and that little bottle of Screech, I am once more with those marvellous skippers of the outports and the drink is flowing and the Atlantic gale is rattling the clapboards outside.

There is the heady smell of clam chowder wafting though from the kitchen and the sound and the unmistakable aroma of fish tongues sizzling on the old blackleaded stove, smells and sounds that are so much a part of Newfoundland to me and which make me hungry right now to think of them.

A wrinkled old gnome of a man is pumping away at the squeeze-box and iron-shod boots are stomping around the plank floor and the good old Newfie songs are getting a raucous airing and the family cat is curled up on the stool by the hearth and blissfully sleeping away through it all ....

Nostalgia doesn't get any more nostalgic than this.

CHAPTER SIXTEEN

Timothy of the Big Water

The indigenes call it the 'Big Water', and it is an apt name. The River Niger's source is close to the boundary of Sierra Leone, then it wends its way eastward for over two thousand miles until, in the savannah lands near Timbuktu, it arcs its way southward, becoming ever wider and deeper until, suddenly, it breaks into pieces to form the many outlets that make up the Niger Delta away to the south of the old trading post of Lokoja.

It was this latter part of Lokoja southward that I got to know particularly well, and it was here that I got to know Timothy of the Big Water. Timothy was jet-black, ugly as sin, and practically rotund. He was of that irrepressible Ijaw tribe, the famous watermen of southern Nigeria, and he was one of the happiest Africans I have ever known.

When I first met him, he was working as a medical orderly on the Asaba to Onitsha ferry. A smallpox epidemic had broken out locally and, to keep it from spreading, the Nigerian

Government had appointed Timothy to vaccinate everyone who came on board. This most emphatically included yours truly, for I was crossing twice daily – to Onitsha in the morning, then back to Asaba in the afternoon. As a result, I got more than my share of vaccinations, for I was vaccinated each time I stepped aboard that damned ferry. By the end of my first fortnight, both my arms were covered in scabs. Timothy made light of my protestations. He told me that I should be flattered that he was using me as an example to the others; the locals were terrified of needles, so when they saw a European baring his arm at Timothy's request, it did his street-cred a power of good. They reckoned that if his juju was good enough for a white man, it was good enough for them.

When I got to know him better, he told me that he had purchased his medical certificate from Kaka Balogun, Master Forger of Benin City. Mr Balogun cranked them out on a little machine on a daily basis at five Nigerian shillings a time. Timothy's only regret was that he did not have an extra ten shillings in his possession then, for the enterprising Mr Balogun could have qualified him as a gynaecologist at the same time.

Timothy was proud of his hygiene. He used a sewing needle for scratching his patients' arms for the application of the vaccine, and he kept this needle in the lapel of his jacket. To make absolutely sure that it was clean, however, he would give it a precautionary licking with his great blue, giraffe-like tongue before putting it to use on each patient. We did not, thank God, know anything about AIDS and such horrors back in those days, but I have to confess that I still have a queasy feeling whenever I think about those Niger River crossings.

The two main towns on the western section of this southern part of the Big Water are Lokoja to the north and Asaba to the south. On the eastern bank, we have Idah and

Onitsha. Onitsha was the great Nigerian literary town of my day. The place fascinated me, for it was to here that all of Nigeria's weirdos came to spout poems and to relate their loopy stories to drunken audiences. The Onitsha Printing Press churned out their various outpourings inside the covers of little red booklets which were sold throughout Nigeria at one shilling and sixpence per copy, excellent value for the money. The Onitsha Printing Press, in fact, printed anything that guaranteed them at least one penny profit. One enormously popular booklet was entitled: *Advice to Lovers. How to snare your girl by writing her a decent Love Letter.* I immediately purchased a copy, for at the time I felt that I was badly in need of some advice in this direction. I opened it at Page One.

'Darling Moonshine of my Sole,' it began, sensibly getting down to the nitty-gritty straightaway and skipping all the boring formalities of foreplay, 'I need you as much as I need my daily cassava and my eventide jug of palm wine. My wives are like Cock Roaches compared to the climax love I feel for you. My thoughts of you are priceless ones.

'Bed is a lonely place without you, my Darling. And I feel as the dessert Bedwin must feel without his favourite Drumaderry to give him solace.

'I await your reply with feverish loins.

'May God have mussy on your sole.

'Your lovelorn sooter,

'Amen to this Himm of Love.'

There was a postscript to this rubbish:

'Put only 4 kisses at the end of this first letter,' advised the author, 'in case she thinks you are being too promiseterous. You must be careful to protect your Good Name, for if she rejects you, you will want to fry another fish.'

This was heady stuff indeed. I placed the booklet in my bag for future reference. One day, I reckoned, I might very well wish to find myself a fish to fry.

I asked Timothy of the Big Water how many wives he had.

'Twelve-and-a-half,' he replied.

'Twelve and a what?' I exclaimed in puzzlement.

'A half,' he reiterated. 'The half one is only a part-time wife. She only comes in when the others are out working on my farm. In fact she is on board the ferry today. I'll introduce her to you.'

She was, in fact, a very pretty little thing. She was of a delicate café-au-lait hue, typical of the Jekri tribe from which she hailed and she had a smile that would have melted the heart of a wooden god. Her birth-given name was Jinty, she said, but all her friends called her Half-Wife, and she would be pleased if I would call her that, too.

She was full of fun, and she was full of ribald, hilarious stories about being a part-time member of Timothy's harem. Ferry journeys suddenly became a lot more bearable, despite Timothy's mania for vaccinations. All of a sudden, I acquired a lot more scabs on my arms.

Timothy's medical career, though, ended as quickly as it had begun. The smallpox epidemic died out. Timothy, in any case, was not too bothered. He had developed a hankering for life on the Big Water waves. Half-Wife informed me that as soon as he could save up for a deposit on a sturdy canoe, he would start up business taking passengers to the little riverside villages that the big ferry couldn't reach. Half-Wife had no difficulty in bumming the necessary twenty pounds from me.

It suited me, anyway, for I was mapping the villages along the Big Water at the time, and I certainly had to go to places on occasion that the government ferry was unable to reach. Sometimes, I even stayed at one of Timothy's houses on the outskirts of Lokoja, where his gaggle of delightful wives fussed over me like a brood of clucking hens over a favourite chick. Half-Wife was also sometimes there. Indeed, on my first night, observing an admirable old Nigerian custom, Timothy offered me her services for the night to keep me 'from getting a chill in bed, for you will remember, sir, that this is the time of the harmattan, when the nights get a little parky.' But although I was young and supremely fit in those days I was also incredibly naïve and innocent, so the closest poor Half-Wife got to me was when she served me breakfast at the table the following morning.

It took her the best part of a year to forgive me for that.

~~~~~

The mighty Niger had had its share of explorers and adventurers. The most famous of the explorers was undoubtedly Mungo Park, a countryman of mine. He drowned at the Bussa rapids, to the north of Lokoja, while being attacked by tribesmen from the high cliffs above. Clapperton and Lander completed Park's work in 1826 by tracing the course of the Niger to the sea. There was a poignant little twist to this whole episode when one of Mungo Park's sons went out to West Africa in quest of his father. (To the end of her life, Mungo Park's wife believed that her husband was still alive.) The son plunged into the bush around Lokoja and was never heard of again.

When I went out myself around the 1950s to do a modest survey of the same area, I found a legend common among the local fishermen about a spectral canoe that could be seen on clear harmattan nights in the middle of the river, a bearded white man sitting in it, paddling determinedly downriver. On certain nights no fisherman could be persuaded to paddle these waters, for to come upon this image meant death by drowning.

I tried not to go out in the middle of the Big Water myself by night, either, but it wasn't the possibility of meeting phantom canoemen that bothered me. Great islands of floating sudd would quite often be encountered day and night drifting downstream, particularly on the approach of the rains. At night these could be a horrible nuisance, for they were so low-lying that the river voyager would be in among the dense vegetation before he realised he was in trouble.

The sudd consisted of a loosely bound tangle of papyrus, grass, water-weeds, water-lilies, water-hyacinth and rushes. When viewed by daylight, in fact, these islands of sudd were quite attractive. Lilies and hyacinth were predominant, and their white and blue flowers sparkled prettily in the full glare of the sunshine. Jacanas – or lily-trotters, as they were more commonly called – walked sedately over the lily pads, their long spidery feet spread out and keeping them from sinking. From a distance, it gave them the appearance of walking on water. They were plover-sized in body, and two were carrying chicks under their wings, the long straggly legs of the chicks being the only visible part of them.

Once, I had to go out on the river by night for some now-forgotten reason with a canoeman and – sure enough – we got stuck on one of these blessed islands of sudd. We spent the best part of two hours hacking away with machetes to clear ourselves, sweating and cursing and being assailed by clouds of mosquitoes. By the time we got out of the stuff we had drifted far downstream, and it was dawn before we had paddled back to Lokoja.

My work finished on the Big Water and I was called further inland to do some work around the Choka-Choka Hills, fifty miles to the west of Lokoja. Opportunities for getting into town were limited, and I lost track of Timothy for a couple of years. But I heard the occasional rumour, for the bush telegraph is very active in Nigeria's interior. He had become, it was said, a highly important chief and politician in the area, with a colossal mansion up in the cool hills overlooking Lokoja. Apart from musing to myself that the ferry business must be a very lucrative one on the Niger, and wondering if, one day, I would get my twenty quid back, I gave the matter no further thought.

There came a day, however, when I found myself standing on the beach below Lokoja, idly watching a great island of sudd floating slowly past. A nudge in the small of my back made me turn round. 'Good God! Half-Wife!' I exclaimed.

She was as beautiful as ever, but *very* opulent looking. Her dark-blue dress looked like some Parisian creation, and her neck and wrists glittered with silver and gold and just about all the rubies of Asia. We chatted excitedly about old times and she told me that Timothy of the Big Water was now a big man in the new Nigerian Parliament.

'I never realised,' I said, 'when you borrowed that twenty pounds from me, that Niger ferrying would be so lucrative, or I might have kept the money and gone into business myself.'

Her explosion of laughter made the riverside jacanas rise

in a flurry of protest. 'Good God, Don,' she declared. 'He didn't make his money through ferrying. Ferrying is a miserably poor way to try to make a living.'

'Then how....?'

'Diamond smuggling, of course!'

'Diamond smuggling!' I exclaimed in horror.

'Yes, I thought a smart guy like you would have cottoned on to that. It was all the rage back then. He employed me to pick up the diamonds over in Liberia, and from there I crossed country by mammy-wagon through the savannah to Lokoja. Here, they were checked over by Timothy, then sent by his canoe-ferry to Onitsha, where they were picked up by courier for onward transport to Douala. They were still in their rough state, but they were worth a hell of a lot of money.'

'How did you avoid getting caught?' I asked.

'Oh, I came close to it a few times,' she said. 'But a young good-looking woman always knows how to buy her way out of a tight corner when dealing with men.'

'Timothy had dropped the smuggling racket now?' I asked nervously.

Her smile was as enigmatic as her reply.

'He is a politician, Don,' she reminded me.

I was speechless. I gazed out over the Big Water, over the island of sudd, watching the lily-trotters at play with their youngsters. She spoke again:

'You see, Monsieur Don, what you missed out on? If you had made me your Half-Wife when you had the chance back then you would have been the richest man on the Big Water by now.

'Yes, Half-Wife,' I replied. 'Or with my luck, probably the richest man in the Lagos Penitentiary.'

She favoured me with her most expansive smile.

'Would I have been worth it?' she asked mischievously.

'For that beautiful smile,' I replied, 'I think that any red-blooded man would have risked Death-Row itself.'

Her eyes sparkled with merriment.

'I thought you would say something like that,' she said, 'for you always were an old-world gentleman. Sometimes too much so.'

She linked her arm through mine.

'Let's go and see if Timothy of the Big Water has any wine for us,' she said, 'and I'm sure he'll want you to stay the night for old-times' sake.'

We walked up the beach in the sunshine. The weaver-birds sang in the coconut palms as they stitched their intricate nests together. Their normal harsh chatter, I noted, had been replaced by melodies more in keeping with what they were doing. Theirs was the sweet, musical trill of the mating song.

It was the start of the African dry season, and the air seemed to crackle with that strange, busy sort of excitement that always hits the inhabitants of the Big Water at this time of the year.

CHAPTER SEVENTEEN

Happy Valley

I was sitting with a Tiv hunter called Dammit in the middle of a sea of savannah scrub a few years after Nigeria had cast off her colonial shackles for good. He was telling me ghost stories.

Tivs are very good at telling ghost stories, for their race is steeped in the supernatural. They are also an exceedingly blood-thirsty race. In my time their favourite weapon was a miniature version of a longbow, a rather innocuous looking thing on first sight, truth be told. But it was the arrows the curdled the blood. The iron heads were razor sharp, viciously barbed so that they were virtually impossible to pull out of the flesh, and they were tipped with the most unpleasant poison known to man, the 'breakback poison'. This was a viscous substance obtained from the seeds of the 'Breakback Tree' (*Dichapetalum* species), a common tree hereabouts. It is a poison whose effect is very similar to that of strychnine, in that, in his final excruciating throes, the victim's back bends backwards until the back of his head touches his heels and his backbone snaps. The tiniest scratch from an arrow tipped with this horrid poison, and you were history within seconds.

No one of nervous disposition ever went to sleep easily after incurring the wrath of a Tiv.

But I liked old Dammit. I was, at that time, in the employ of a Californian consortium who had hired me to do a survey on the little pockets of 'kurimé' forest that dotted this charming part of Northern Nigeria. The kurimé were seldom more than two square miles in area, always found near to water or with water running though them, and scattered all over the scrub savannah. They were havens of shelter for bush cow, elephant, antelope, monkeys, and the like, for they consisted, in the main, of heavy-crowned species of tree such as fig, ako, ekki and obeche, and, in season, they were veritable gardens of fruit and wild yams. Dammit knew this area like the back of his hand, so I had hired him as my guide.

We were sitting on the verge of the Choka-Choka, a cluster of low-lying hills about halfway between the old cattle town of Kabba to the west and the even more ancient town of Lokoja, fifty miles to the east on the juncture of the Niger and Benué rivers. In the middle of the Choka-Choka, the old man told me, there was a secret glen about five miles long called the Valley of Eternal Happiness. It was full of animals, each one of which, he believed, was the reincarnation of a departed Tiv, and it was to this Valley that those of his ancestors who had behaved themselves in life were allowed to go to spend an eternity of tranquillity. This, he further informed me, was the spiritual home of Nigeria's phantom elephant Old Toby.

I pricked up my ears at this information, for the legend of Old Toby was well known to me. Indeed, it was well known to many even outwith the borders of Nigeria. I had, myself, come upon what was reputed to be the legend's spoor from time to time in the wilderness surrounding the Choka-Choka Hills. The footprints were by far the largest I had ever seen of any elephant. He was obviously huge and his tusks were so large that it was said he had to rest them on the ground every few hundred yards, so heavy were they. His fame was such that white hunters from as far away as Kenya had taken the long trip overland to Nigeria to try to bag him. None had succeeded in getting even a glimpse of the giant; nothing but those massive footprints did they ever see and the indentation of those enormous tusks in the soil to tease them.

There were very good reasons as to why Old Toby should have survived for so long, Dammit told me. For one thing, no bullets could harm him, for when any shot was fired at him, the bullet would divert in its flight and fly over the top of him. Also, although he went walkabout on the odd occasion, the Valley of Eternal Happiness was his ancestral home, the place to which he always returned and the Valley was a sacred place. It was guarded by the Fever Bird, which soared ceaselessly over the entrance to the Valley, protecting its inmates. Anyone who entered the Valley with evil intentions towards the animals would not live long to tell the tale. The Fever Bird would see them, and exact terrible retribution.

'If you insist upon going into the Valley with me,' warned the old man, 'leave your shotgun behind in my house. The animals are our friends. We won't need meat. There are plenty of wild yams we can dig up in the kurimé, so we won't starve.'

The Valley of Eternal Happiness was well named. An aura of peace seemed to settle over my shoulders the moment I entered it. The ten days I spent with Dammit in its verdant glades were most pleasant ones. The little patches of kurimé were alive with birdsong and the happy chatter of vervet monkeys. Troupes of baboons were everywhere, their cheek pouches bulging with the green fruit of the savannah opépé, their street-wise eyes thoughtful as they watched us pass by. Once, we came upon a small family of the little red bushpig, the cute little piglets snuffling and snorting and squeaking along at their mothers' heels. In the evenings, our campsite would invariably be visited by the fairy flycatcher, surely the most beautiful of all birds. Camp fires seemed to have a peculiar fascination for this bird, and it would hover over the glowing embers, its wings a blur, in an absolute delectation of shimmering blues and silvers, quite unafraid of us. We even saw a family of rare pygmy elephants in a small patch of kurimé. We never set eyes on Old Toby, but we came upon what Dammit said was his spoor and droppings around the fringe of a tiny swamp where tall yellow lilies waltzed together in a gentle zephyr in the cool of the evening. In such a setting, even my enforced vegetarian diet did not irk as much as it might otherwise have done.

Our contentment was interrupted by the surprise arrival of a sweating African lad with a note for me, a note, quite literally, held in a cleft stick. He was, he said, an official government 'runner', and he had been commissioned by a white man staying in the Kabba government rest house to carry this message to me. Somewhat puzzled, I unfolded the piece of paper.

'Come at once to see me,' it ordered in peremptory fashion. 'Instructions of Chief Festus Okotie Eboh.' It was signed 'Hiram J. Parker Jr'.

I had no idea what this could be all about, but I suspected that it wouldn't mean very good news for me. I hadn't a clue who Hiram J. Parker Jr was, but everyone knew that Chief Festus Okotie Eboh was Bad News, in capital letters at that. Officially Minister of Finance in the Nigerian Government, he was a singularly nasty bit of work. I had met him once, some months previously and he looked as obnoxious as his reputation; an obese slug of a man, brutal, repugnant, corrupt to an incredible degree, even by the West African standards of the day. Penniless before his election he was now, it was said, worth half a billion dollars, most of it deposited in secret bank accounts in Switzerland. As far as I was concerned, that was all he was worth. It was with a sense of deep foreboding that I walked out of the Valley of Eternal Happiness, accompanied by the faithful Dammit.

As it turned out, I did not like the look of Hiram J. Parker much more than I had liked the look of Chief Festus Okotie Eboh. Most Americans, I have found to be warm, generous to a fault, and always out to please, but this one was loud, brash and rude. He was short and fat, with a porcine face, and he was clad in what he obviously considered to be *de rigueur* for a Great White Hunter: cream-coloured corduroy jodhpurs, a coral-pink shirt, a damask bush-jacket with shining gold buttons, and a Sam Browne-type belt bristling with cartridges. He had a pearl-handled Colt revolver at his hip, and in his hand he was ostentatiously holding a brand new Holland and Holland elephant rifle which had obviously yet to fire its first shot.

Everything about him smelled of wealth, and I had never seen a more ridiculous-looking human being in my life.

For some reason known to himself and whatever Gods Americans worship, he began our relationship by calling me 'Monty'. More offensively, he made an even poorer start with Dammit by calling him 'Sambo' and ignoring the Tiv's outstretched welcoming hand. He showed me his introduction from Chief Festus Okotie Eboh. It stated that Mr Hiram J. Parker Jr was a noted American sportsman who was to be given all assistance in shooting whatever animals he wanted and in particular in the area known as the Valley of Eternal

Happiness in the Kabba Province of Northern Nigeria. I was horrified. Two things were immediately apparent to me, viz: the American must have concluded a satisfactory monetary deal with the corrupt Minister to have been given authority to shoot in such a hallowed area, and secondly, what he was really after was Old Toby's tusks.

I demurred: 'The locals won't like it. This area is sacred to them.'

He replied brusquely: 'I don't give a fuck whether these black monkeys like it or not. I'm going in, and neither you nor they can stop me.'

Then he threw off all pretence.

'I hear there's a real big tusker in there, and I'm going to get him.'

'Then,' I informed him, 'you won't have me for company.'

'I'll soon get company,' he sneered. 'Money means every-thing to these monkeys.'

He brought out his wallet and fished out an impressive fistful of bills, waving them in Dammit's face.

'Doesn't it Sambo?'

Dammit stared at him coldly.

'I make enough from my normal hunting to satisfy me,' he said. 'I don't need your filthy cash.'

The American's face turned puce.

'You ugly black bastard!' he spluttered. 'I'll report you to the honourable Okotie Eboh.'

'You can report me to the devil in hell, if you like,' replied the imperturbable Dammit. 'I'm sure I would find even he to be more honourable than giaours like you and Okotie Eboh.'

It was when the American raised his fist that I knew that the situation had got out of hand. I sprang in between them and grabbed his wrist. I am very slow to anger, as even those who don't have cause to like me much would no doubt admit, but now I was seething.

'Let's get one thing clear right now, sonny boy,' I hissed in his face. 'Okotie Eboh can't help you now for he's far away in Lagos. Either you mind your manners while you are with me or I'll shove that pretty little shotty-gun of yours where the sun never shines and pull the trigger.'

He glared at me for a long moment, his face suffused with fury. Then he relaxed and shrugged his shoulders.

'Okay, Monty,' he said. 'No point in getting all steamed up about it. I'll go into town and hire some people myself to take into the Valley. Every man has his price. Even you, Monty. I just haven't had time to work on you properly yet.'

He returned a few hours later with half-a-dozen sullen-looking youths. He also had with him two young damsels who could by no stretch of the imagination have been termed porters, decked out as they were in the most modern 'Lagos-gear': the briefest of mini-skirts, scarlet lipstick, violet eye-shadow, all the trimmings. He asked me if he could borrow my bed for an hour and I could see that my emphatic 'No!' had not softened his opinion of me. Minutes later the whole lot of them were off down the hill, the porters with his loads on their heads and Hiram J. Parker Jr trailing behind with his girls.

When they had gone I produced a bottle of lager from the kerosene refrigerator in the rest house and placed it before Dammit. Then I gave him some money.

'Now,' I explained, 'I'll have to leave for Lagos today to report this new development to my chiefs, for I fear that there is going to be trouble with this white man. I don't expect to be back here for about a fortnight. I want you to give Mr Parker and his people a day's start then take a bush taxi to the Choka-Choka and follow them into the Valley to make sure that they don't get into trouble. If there is trouble of any kind, come straight out and report it to the Kabba district officer. He is a Hausa and he is my friend. He will know what to do. And whatever you do, keep well out of sight of them. I do not want them to know that you are following them. I do not trust that white man.'

Leaving him to mull over this stricture, I went off to pack my bag for the long trip to Lagos.

I returned after ten days or so to find Kabba swarming with police and the whole town buzzing like a nest of hornets on marijuana. Commissioner of Police, Englishman George Duckett, was waiting for me in the rest house. I had known George for quite some time, and we were friends. Nearer to seven feet in height than six, he was one of those old-fashioned policemen who actually looked like a policeman and not like some pallid male mannequin.

While I was away, he told me, he had been on one of his periodic official tours of the Province. In Kabba town, he said, a black man called Dammit had approached him to report that a white man was shooting everything that moved in the Choka-Choka area. The locals were getting very shirty over it and he – Dammit – was afraid that there was trouble brewing. Therefore, following my instructions, he had come out to seek help.

George had hurried into the Valley with his small band of policemen. There they had found the weirdly contorted body of Hiram J. Parker Jr, lying in the open, surrounded by baboons, who were eating lumps out of the corpse. The baboons were most aggressive, said he, and he had had to shoot three of them to get at the body.

'You shot three of the baboons?' I asked worriedly.

'Yes. Why?' he queried suspiciously

'Nothing,' I said. 'Nothing at all. Just a foolish superstition the local hunters have.'

He asked me to accompany him to the top of an inselberg overlooking the Valley so that we could get an overall view of it and he could point out the spot where the body had been found. Dammit, he said, had disappeared, and no one had set eyes upon him since he had delivered his report.

'But you know what these blighters are like,' remarked the policeman philosophically. 'They hate the police, and they have a great fear of being involved in anything unpleasant. So they just bugger off into the bush.'

At the top of the inselberg he stopped and scanned the Valley below with his binoculars. Suddenly, he tensed and handed them to me.

'Have a look at that,' he said. 'At the far end of the Valley.'

I peered through them. 'Good God, Old Toby!' I gasped. 'It must be Old Toby!'

Pulling leaves from a tree in the distance was the biggest elephant I had ever seen in my life. Even allowing for slight distortion from the mist slowly rolling down the Valley, I would have estimated his tusks to be around nine feet in length. I had never seen such magnificence. We watched for a long time, and he was the only living thing we saw in the Valley that day. But I was satisfied.

George put his binoculars away. We turned to work our way back down the inselberg. From high overhead, a wild, eerie scream made us look up sharply. A great, vulture-like bird was soaring high over the Valley; vulture-like, but absolutely enormous.

George began to unclip his binocular case, but by the time he had them out, the mist had blotted everything from view. In some haste, we scrambled down the slope to the road. High above us, its form hidden from view by the swirling banks of fog, the demoniac screams of that strange creature echoed throughout the bluffs surrounding the Valley of Eternal Happiness.

That, really, is the end of my story. I left Nigeria shortly after. The darker secrets of the Valley will die with me. However, I am permitted to tell you those that are already known to at least a few outside the Valley: Old Toby was never seen by human eyes again, and Dammit vanished forever into the bush of his tribal homeland. As for the others, the Ibadan pathologist said that Hiram J. Parker Jr had been killed by some strychnine-like substance. The body had been too badly mutilated by animals to determine by what means the poison had been administered. Some time later, George Duckett was assassinated by a .22 rifle bullet fired from the darkness of his compound while attending to a defective electric light bulb on the verandah of his new Caribbean home. Around the same time, Chief Festus Okotie Eboh was bludgeoned to death at his Lagos home by army officers during a military coup.

Make of all that what you will. For myself, I have no sensible theories to offer.

CHAPTER EIGHTEEN

Marie of Roumania

Oh, life is a glorious cycle of song,
A medley of extemporanea;
And love is a thing that can never go wrong;
And I am Marie of Roumania.

Dorothy Parker

'WIFE DECAPITATES HUSBAND'S PENIS WITH ONE BITE IN DOMESTIC TIFF' screamed the front page of the *Nigeria Daily Times* with obvious relish. It continued: 'In fit of pique, husband shears wife's pubic region with Swiss Army knife.' Both plaintiffs had to exhibit their maimed private parts to an enthralled and packed courtroom at the divorce hearing.

'I think,' remarked Chief Justice Lawson Olubandere with commendable understatement, 'that we may take it that love is waning in this particular marriage.'

Post-Independence, the Nigerian press had become a constant source of amusement for us expatriates. One riffled through screeds of political waffle to get to that vital piece of entertainment, but, when found, it generally proved to be well worth the effort. Newspapers tried to match the excesses of the English tabloids, particularly the more prurient ones, and they often proved to be more than a match for them. The *Drum Magazine* became, for some of us, favourite Sunday morning reading, and the agony-aunt page, particularly so.

'Dear Dolly,' wrote one perplexed African lady, 'my husband is a chief in Abeokuta. We are both 94 years of age. Until now, he has been very content with our marriage. It has been normal. Every night, when he has had his bowl of rice, he forks me. Then he buggers off to his own bed. But now he is content no more, for he has started reading European rubbish. He wants different kinds of love making. So, I need this advice from you, dear Dolly. When I am about to give him oral sex, should I remove my false teeth?'

However, such refinements in the relations between the sexes had not yet arrived on the Coast when I first went out to the White Man's Grave. The kiss was unknown, and the only kind of sex was heterosexual. But one never, ever, saw a man and girl walking hand in hand together. (Curiously enough, it was quite common to see two male youths walking hand in hand together, but that was always a male-bonding thing. Homosexuality was unknown. Later on, homosexuality was to take a firm root in seats of learning such as the Lagos and Ibadan universities, brought in via European contact.)

Around the 8th century BC, that arch chauvinist Hesiod the Greek wrote that man should never marry, for that gave women ideas above their station in life. Women, he asserted, were mere breeding machines, gifted by a benevolent God to the male of the species for the production of children who would look after her lord and master in his dotage. In between those essential tasks, he wrote, if it was obvious to him that time was hanging heavy on her hands, he could always put her out to the plough.

The West African male I knew in those early days would have got on just fine with the old Greek curmudgeon. He knew where a woman's place was, and that was away down among the scullions. The very thought of being nice to his nearest and dearest would have given him a fit of the vapours. Female babies had their value, for they produced a good dowry for their father when their time came to marry, but a boy child was their pride and joy. The boy was the potential big-money earner, for if he were smart enough, he would be educated, become a doctor, a lawyer, a politician. No one would think of educating a girl. Wasted money. She was destined to become a skivvy to her father and her future husband.

The barbarism of female circumcision was still in vogue when I went out to the Coast for the first time. Not all tribes practised it, but many did so. The Sobo males of Benin seemed to have a particular relish for it. There was, in my opinion, only one reason for the continuation of this horrible practice – the sheer bloody-mindedness of the menfolk. It was perpetrated purely and simply to deny their women any pleasure at all from the sexual act. I have never, thanks be to God, seen the operation being performed, but I have seen the tools of the trade. The favourite implement consisted of a rusting jagged shard of tin hacked from a redundant kerosene drum. The operation was performed around puberty by one of the tribe's matriarchs, and a singularly messy and painful one it proved to be. Needless to say, the only anaesthetic was that which was provided by the filthy dregs of ancient kerosene still smeared to the blade.

I once asked a Sobo intellectual why his tribe still persisted with this awful custom. His reply simply confirmed all my views on this intrinsically crabbit and supremely chauvinistic tribe:

'American ranchers brand their cattle to show who they

belong to. We brand our women by circumcising them.'

There was a strange ambivalence about the average male West African's approach to sex. He liked it, but he was going to make damned sure that his woman didn't enjoy it too much, otherwise she might stray. He didn't mind sharing his wife with a close friend when it suited him, and indeed – being at heart a generous sort of chap – he quite often did.

When a man was down on his luck and out of sorts, his tribal chief could often be relied upon to lend him one of his younger wives for a month or so to help him through his depression. This, it was reasoned, was after all what tribal chiefs were for. In any case, if the chief was a big enough shot, he would have wives in abundance. One of my friends, a small-time cocoa farmer, had thirteen wives, and he was looking forward to the day when he was a big enough farmer to be able to afford fifty of them, so that he could lend some out to his friends when he felt like showing off a bit.

In some of the more remote areas, though, the number of wives a chief had was not always what mattered most to him. Often, much more important to him was the number of cows and goats he possessed.

Many years ago, while I was living on the outskirts of the charming little village town of Ado-Ekiti in Nigeria, I was befriended by an old Hausa trader, Baba Kano. I had done him a minor favour, and in return he gave me a massive, very heavy bronze bracelet. It was obviously very old, with strange markings engraved into the bronze. He informed me that it was an ancient type of currency called 'manilla'. Each Nigerian kingdom, he said, had its own size of currency, with its own engravings, and the one I had in my hand now was that of his own kingdom, the Hausa Kingdom. I asked the old man what it had been worth in the old days.

'One cow, or twenty women,' he replied, without a hint of badinage in his voice.

Around Independence Day in 1960, on the Coast, there appeared the phenomenon called the Ladies of the Night. This was a phenomenon aimed solely at the white man, for the black man had not the slightest interest in prostitutes, at least, not in black ones. In coastal towns, if you went into a bar on a hot day for a cold drink, you knew that you would be accosted by swarms of very pretty black girls. They were always as happy and chattery as a flock of weaverbirds, each vying for your undivided attention. Initially, those accommodating ladies were to be found only in the air-conditioned comfort of the coastal towns, and it took time for them to venture too far upcountry, but venture inland they eventually did. Suddenly, in remote areas where young whites were sweating their lives away in conditions that would not be tolerated today, randy young males had more to occupy their minds and bodies than endless games of cribbage and tennis in the local expatriate club.

In our British colonial system, it was all very discreet, of course. No hanky-panky; at least, not so the outside world would notice, anyway.

There was a fair amount of truth in the old Paddy Roberts song of those times:

The Englishman is noted for his 'sang froid',
Which, translated, means his usual bloody cold;
He likes his pipe and slippers,
And the missus and the nippers,
And he's happy simply growing old.
And the slightest demonstration of affection,
He regards as being rather infra dig;
He thinks the way the French behave is absolutely nuts;
He'd like to try it, really, but he doesn't have the guts;

He's scared to death the neighbours might be told –
The Englishman with his usual bloody cold.'

The French flaunted their mistresses; we British were supposed to be too refined for such ostentation. For the Brit to act in such a louche way could very well mean his being shovelled onto the next boat home, never to be allowed to return. 'Gone Native' was a term of the deepest disapprobation, and – greatest punishment of all – could get you barred from your local Expatriate Club.

I was mercifully free from such problems. I lived a life that no other white man lived much of the time, far into the gloom of the interior forests, far from the attractions of the expatriate club routine, and all too rarely did temptation fall my way. Indeed, a lot of the time I lived with the despised 'natives', and I wouldn't have had it any other way. They were, in fact, more fun to be with than most of the Club habitués. On the rare occasion that temptation did cross my path, I was generally far too tired after my hard day's toil to raise the energy, if that is the appropriate phrase, to succumb to it. But there was one incident that comes vividly to mind whenever I think of Africa and her temptations.

I was living in a Lugard bungalow on the European Reservation in the old trading town of Lokoja. My houseboy, Peter, was a lovely Ibo lad with an unfortunate stutter. He had been my faithful companion for fifteen years or so. I was sitting back in my armchair, enjoying my first beer of the day. He entered, and stood before me.

'There's a Hoo…Hoo….Hoo…' he gurgled, then tailed off into a gasping silence, his mouth opening and closing wordlessly like that of a bullfrog with a grasshopper stuck in its throat.

I waited politely, and he tried again.

'There's a Hoo… Hoo…. Hoo… Back door,' he ended with an impotent stutter.

I took a sip at my beer while he gathered himself together for a shit-or-bust effort. It took time, but out it came eventually: 'Hoo… Hoo… Whore from Lagos at back door!!' he roared triumphantly.

Now, whores from the big city were as rare as white giraffes in my neck of the woods in those early Nigerian days. We had not yet become civilised enough for that. Bush amateurs were ten a penny, but city professionals? This sounded like the start of a new era for me. I looked at Peter. His eyes, I thought, shone with a new light. Devotion was there, but then devotion had always been there. Now, there was an additional something, a new glow, but what could it be? Ah yes, if I was not badly mistaken, it was sheer pride. Massa, he was convinced, had made it at last. His young Master was about to prove his Manhood, and with a Whore from Lagos, no less; the Premier League of whores. I followed him silently down the back steps, through the kitchen, out to the back door. A quite extraordinary sight met my eyes.

She was tall, long-limbed, of café-au-lait colouring, extremely good-looking, and of obvious Nilotic stock. But there, her resemblance to those aristocratic Fulanis from the far north ended, for she was clad from head to toe in cowboy gear. A large pink Stetson adorned her head, her frilled top was of the most expensive buckskin, her skin-tight trousers were of a delicate cream shade, and her scarlet leather cowboy boots had attached to them great silver spurs with vicious-looking rowels. A pair of pearl-handled toy revolvers hung from a leather belt slung around her shapely hips and, in her left hand, she carried a very business-like riding crop.

'I am Betsy, the whore from Lagos,' she announced as I stood there open-mouthed. She flicked her whip, its sharp crack making me wince involuntarily.

'I am for white men only,' she continued proudly. 'Five pounds per night for ordinary romps in bed, and two pounds extra for deviations, such as if you want me to wear my spurs and use my whip on you while we are doing it. I can also offer you my Special, which was much remarked upon in Lagos. It is called, 'Betsy's Sexual Rodeo', for which you will need to clear all furniture except the bed out of the room, for we will require plenty of space to manoeuvre during this one.'

A large ebony elephant carving acting as a doorstop behind her received a hefty whack on its rump with the whip for emphasis, the painful-sounding crack making Peter scurry back to the sanctuary of the living room with a yelp of alarm, his honest black face turning a curious shade of hodden-grey as he departed.

I gave her a cold beer and dismissed her as politely as I could. I watched her as she went off down the garden path. She was, she had said, going to try her luck with the Resident in the next compound. She felt it in her bones that she would have more luck there, for she had heard that the Resident was an English gentleman of the old school who would appreciate class when he saw it. I could see that she meant her words to sting, too.

I felt a pang of regret as I watched her go. With her sense of theatre, she deserved a more appreciative audience than me. But who knows, I thought. Perhaps the Resident and his Lady might even enjoy a whack at Betsy's Sexual Rodeo. It would at least be an educational experience, I felt sure, for I doubted if it would be something they practised on a regular basis around the old Residency four-poster.

CHAPTER NINETEEN

Drums Along
the Mahogany Trail

She closed her eyes; and in sweet slumber lying,
Her spirit tiptoed from its lodging place.
It's folly to shrink in fear, if this is dying;
For death looked lovely in her lovely face.

Francesco Petrarca

As graves go, you couldn't find a more beautiful spot for it in all of Africa. Especially in the dry season, for then the lemon bush casting its shade over it is at its most bountiful, its slender branches covered in large, bright-yellow fruit, while the giant silver-barked obeche trees, towering a couple of hundred feet high all around, have shed their multi-hued maple-like leaves upon it, giving it a thick, warm quilt of quite the prettiest leaves you are liable to find anywhere in the world, for the obeche, unlike most West African rainforest trees, sheds all of its leaves in the dry season.

The grave is situated on the verge of a tiny hamlet called Geeble town, deep in the forest. Unusually too for this part of the world, a concrete tombstone has been erected over it, and on this stone you will find engraved the simple epitaph:

'Here lies Princess Elizabeth Tobey, gone to her final resting place, aged 14 years, January 23rd 1960.'

A dirt track wends its way through cassava farms for ten miles from the main bitumen road to the village. It is a pleasant enough road should you care to take it; that is, provided you keep a weather-eye open for the odd gaboon viper and river-jack at slumber by the side of the track, for these frightful reptiles are among the most venomous snakes in the whole wide world. Should you venture down this track to the grave, don't forget to take with you a bottle of good whisky, for it is only right that you pay your respects in the traditional way to the grave's occupant by pouring a fair libation over her. Even if you don't believe in such old-fashioned courtesies, it will do your street-cred no harm at all around Geeble Town. And anyway, your popularity will reach an all-time high if you share what is left in the bottle with the chief of the village. That, too, is a pleasant old African custom.

It is a good fifty years now since the grave was dug, but you will no doubt find a few old-timers around Geeble town to tell you stories about its occupant. And about me. Stories every-where lose nothing with repeated telling over the passage of time and Africa is no exception. So add a pinch or two of salt as you listen. Especially if the stories are about yours truly. For the grave owes its siting under the lemon tree, and its tombstone, and the lettering on the tombstone, to your humble servant. As for me, although around half-a-century has elapsed since I last saw it, everything about that part of my life leading up to the burial is as clear in my mind now as when I was living it.

But, a final warning: I advise you to move very cautiously when you find yourself in the vicinity of the grave, for it may very well have guardians, and those guardians will be quick to resent intrusion. They will be sharp of fang and claw, I can assure you from painful experience, and they will be all too ready to use both when they get their collective danders up.

She was sitting by the side of the track when I first saw her. She was jet-black in colour, with sparkling eyes, a most un-African pug nose, and a winsome smile. She was wearing a dark-blue top with the logo 'Last of the Dodos' printed in white on the front, and shorts of a vivid scarlet hue, American rubbish purchased at some bush market or other. She was nine years of age, she told me, and her English name was Elizabeth, although most people hereabouts called her 'Cat-Girl'.

She had by her side a pretty, spotted, cat-thing about the size and shape of a Dandy Dinmont dog. I recognised it instantly as being a very young serval cat. I put my hand out to it. It arched its back, spat ferociously, and buried fang and claws deep into the palm of my hand. The Cat-Girl thought it hilarious as I danced up and down in pain, sucking the wounds and cursing profusely.

'She will get used to you,' she comforted me.

Then she queried: 'You are the white man who is coming to stay in our village for a while, aren't you?'

I reassured her on this point and walked with her to the village as my porter followed on behind.

Old Man Tobey was waiting for us. He was the girl's father and chief of the village. He had a hut ready for me, he said, on the edge of the village and right next to the hut in which Elizabeth slept with her two little sisters. I sat next to him outside his hut, sipping palm-wine from a half-coconut shell while I explained to him what I had been sent to do in the area – mapping and timber prospecting.

Elizabeth, he said, had volunteered to wash my clothes and clean out my hut on a daily basis, while one of his wives could prepare my meals. Elizabeth had always 'had a way' with wild animals, he told me, and she had found the 'wild cat' as a kitten in a nest out in the woods and brought it home with her. It never left her side, following her everywhere, even sleeping on her bed. It already did its own hunting, killing rodents and sparrows around the village.

The villagers would all be glad to have me here, he said, particularly if I could take my shotgun out into the woods now and then to kill the occasional antelope or guinea-fowl for them. The village hunter, he said, had been killed by a cobra a week ago, and they had no one else around as yet with sufficient expertise to do the hunting for them.

Suddenly, from behind his hut there came the sound of a drum, loud and sonorous, a BOOM-BOOM-BOOM of sound that echoed out through the trees. I glanced sideways at the old chief.

'We are having a dance tonight in your honour,' he explained, 'and my drummer is telling all the villages around about so that they can come to it.'

As suddenly as it had started, the drumming behind us stopped. Old Man Tobey cupped a hand to his ear.

'Listen!' he commanded.

From far off through the trees came the faint tac-a-tac-a-tac... tac-a-tac-a-tac... tac-a-tac-a-tac of an answering drum.

'That is Jacko Town, telling us that they are sending us their best dancing girls,' he said with the certainty of a man of the forest who, while he would not have recognised his own name printed in big black letters before him, knew the language of the drums by heart. As he spoke, from all points of the compass, from near and far, there came the throb of drumbeats. Old Man Tobey turned to me with a huge grin.

'It's going to be a good night,' he declared with satisfaction.

I went round the back of the hut to have a look at the talking drum. It consisted of a rather crudely hollowed out trunk of the cordia tree, an insignificant forest tree with scaly bark whose light, straw-coloured timber, I was to find out later, was practically the only timber ever used for this purpose because of its incredibly resonating nature when struck.

It was certainly a wonderful night, although my memories of it are a trifle hazy now. Much palm-wine was drunk, and the full moon lit up the village square as bright as day. About halfway through the night I left them to it and staggered off to bed. At God alone knew what time later I became aware of something climbing onto my bed. Remembering the bush African's traditional hospitality with his women, I opened a cautious eye. By the shaft of moonlight spearing through my window I saw the serval cat curling herself up at the foot of my bed...

When I woke in the morning, I had the room to myself. I was cleaning my teeth at the back of the hut when I found the Cat-Girl beside me.

'You had my blanket on your bed last night to keep you warm,' she informed me.

'I suspected something like that,' I replied, 'for I had your cat for company for part of the night.'

She smiled, her lovely eyes twinkling with mischief.

'I hope she didn't scratch you anywhere important?' she asked.

Then, in more serious vein she continued: 'Before you go to work, I want you to do me a favour. Will you please give my cat an English name?'

I had already thought of one.

'Sheba,' I said. 'Sheba was a very beautiful queen long, long ago, and Sheba suits your cat. And now, young Elizabeth, since you, too, are very beautiful and we are in the naming business, from now on I am going to call you 'Princess'.'

She clapped her hands in delight.

'I will be your Princess. Your Princess Elizabeth!' she cackled gleefully.

I looked at her. She was growing up fast. African girls mature quickly. Also, there was a certain look in her eyes whenever she looked at me, that certain look that makes every confirmed bachelor batten the hatches when it is directed at him and weigh anchor with all due celerity if he wishes to stay outwith the blessed bonds of matrimony. For some strange reason I was not unhappy that my work would soon be drawing to a close and I would be spending less and less time around Geeble Town.

The woods around us were alive with game, so shooting for the various pots of the villagers presented few problems for me. Quite often Princess came along with me. I didn't like it much at first for I was always a solitary hunter, but so eager was she to be with me that I relented at last and allowed her to join me on the understanding that she would keep quiet and not frighten the game. Despite her pleading, though, I put a firm bar on Sheba coming with us. I had enough on my plate, I considered, with an eccentric girl in tow, without having to keep a wary eye on a large cat padding along behind me in forests where the unpredictable leopard and the homicidal bush cow held truculent sway.

I shot guinea-fowl, green pigeons, cane rats, duiker antelopes. Once, a dozen red bush-pigs exploded from the thickets around me. A right and a left from my shotgun downed two of the tuskers and the rest disappeared, squealing and snorting, into the undergrowth. The villagers had never fed better, and I think I was the most popular hunter ever, around Geeble town.

But, as the old saw would have it, all good things have to end sometime. My survey was taking me further and further away from the village, and eventually I had to move myself, my porters and my gear far away to a village on the Ivory Coast border. On occasion, I would take a break from work and drive back to Geeble Town. On one of those occasions, when Princess was about thirteen years of age, I arrived to find her in a state of high excitement. Sheba was mother to four kittens. A wild serval from the surrounding bush had been paying court to her at nights, and she had given birth under the wild lemon tree near to Princess's hut. The girl took me to see them. They were tiny bundles of fury, spitting and snarling and raging at me. Remembering my past experience with their mother, I kept my hand well clear of them.

About a year later I was still working over Ivory Coast way when one of those 'cleft-stick messengers' still commonly used in remote parts in my day, tracked me down in the bush. With him, he had a brief note from a hospital doctor to say that

Princess was desperately ill and crying out for me. I downed tools instantly, and arrived at the hospital next day.

The courteous Indian doctor told me that there was little he could do for her except keep pumping pain-killers into her to ease her way towards death. He thought it to be sasswood poisoning for which there was no cure. The father, he said, had told him that he suspected it to have been administered by a spurned lover. The nurse took me through to the ward to see her. Her eyes flickered open as I bent over her and she tried to smile her beautiful Princess smile at me.

She spoke only once before she died.

'Sorry you see me like this, Don,' she whispered. 'But we will meet in another world, and we will go hunting together again. Just you and me together. And Sheba and I will sleep on your bed.'

'It's a deal, my little Princess,' I whispered.

She was holding my hand, still smiling her gentle little smile, when she slipped away from this world and all of its problems.

꙳

My visits to Geeble Town became less and less frequent. There was nothing any more, really, for me to go back to. I paid one final visit shortly before I was due to return to England preparatory to my taking up a teaching post in Newfoundland.

Old Tobey met me. Sheba, he said, had disappeared back into the woods. Her kittens were, of course, fully grown now and they had taken to sleeping on top of the grave under the lemon tree. He wished that I would shoot them for they respected no one and they would not let anyone near the grave. They were devils, he said.

The evening shadows were upon us as I wandered over to the lemon bush. Suddenly I stopped, frozen to the spot. Two large spotted cats, about the size of Doberman pinscher dogs, sat up and glared at me, their eyes glowing coals of hate in the gloom. They bared their fangs at me. I backed off carefully, remembering that I had read somewhere that a peculiarity of the serval species was that generation after generation had been known sometimes to remain in the same territory.

'Princess,' I whispered, 'you are being well looked after. And don't worry – Sheba's family are safe with me.'

Somewhere in the blackness of the forest a talking drum spoke. A second answered, then a third, then a fourth. Suddenly the forests around us were alive with sound. I turned, and walked off to my hut. I just hoped that none of Sheba's family would venture into my bed this night. I was tired, and bed companions were the last thing that I needed.

Especially those whose fangs and claws were capable of wreaking such havoc upon me as their beautiful mother had done such a very long time ago.

CHAPTER TWENTY

La Belle Marguerite

*'The fascination of shooting as a sport
depends almost wholly on whether you
are at the right or wrong end of the gun.'*

P.G. Wodehouse

Beneath the grubby hide of every red-blooded little boy there lies the soul of a hunter-gatherer. Yes, even in this modern era of nano-text-speak gibberish. I am convinced of that. Wrench his ridiculous iPod from his unwashed ears, I maintain, and consign it to the deep along with his twitters and googles and his other electronic madhouse rubbish and he will become a different chap before your very eyes. He will become Normal. Gone will be the zombie who used to creep around your house like a bad dream, scaring Auntie Flo half to death, and putting Gramps Bartholomew clear off his hominy grits. Within the week he will be asking you to let him into the long-lost mystery of how to make catapults and the next-door moggie will be peering warily round corners before it ventures forth to do unpleasant things in your lettuce patch.

I was a country boy, and my parents had very little money. We lived very much off the land. At six years of age, I snared my first rabbit. At six years of age, I was shown by old Jimmy Bell, the farm handyman, how to catch trout by methods that would certainly have raised eyebrows in any decent angling club. At ten years of age, I took the ancient family shotgun out of the house one Christmas Eve, balanced the heavy thing on top of a wall, and blew from the old larch tree at the end of the garden the cock pheasant who had been flaunting his long tail against the light of the moon the past few frosty nights. I am not proud of it now, and the only excuse I have for these outrages is that I have only ever shot for the pot. I have never shot for fun in my life, for I have never derived any fun from taking the life of a wild creature. Sadness, yes, but never joy or satisfaction.

Poverty, wrote Sydney Smith back in 1820, is no disgrace to a man, but it is confoundedly inconvenient. However, it certainly made us children very careful shots. Cartridges were expensive, and it was prudent to make each one count if we were to be allowed to leave the home with the family shotgun. Our father doled out the ammunition as though it contained gold dust instead of lead pellets: four cartridges maximum each time we went out to try to bag a rabbit or a mallard, and each one had to count.

'No target practice at bloody gulls and whaups,' he would warn. 'Shoot only at things that are edible.'

It turned us into adequate shots, for, even in our teenage years, we were a little afraid of the Old Man.

It did not turn me into an enthusiastic shot, though. However, when I went to Africa to work, I soon found that feeding one's crew was very important in the rainforest. A well-fed gang was a happy gang, therefore one of my first appointments when forming a new gang was that of hunter. Although I sometimes carried a shotgun myself, I rarely had to lift it at an animal. Instead, I used it in tree identification. When I came upon a species of tree new to me and which proved difficult to identify, a shot fired into the crown would bring down sufficient leaves and flowers to make precise identification possible. This was about as far as my desire to pull a trigger went. There were some, however, within whom the blood-lust remained strong until the day they died.

I was working among the Guiglo forests of the Ivory Coast. Phillipe, a well-known local character and hunter, had his cabin by the shore of Lac St. Jean, a small sheet of shallow water which harboured myriad migratory wildfowl and a vast variety of game that came down at the end of each day to drink. It was a shooter's paradise.

Phillipe was French. He was short and slight, with skin of a mahogany tan through many years of exposure to the fierce African sun. He was a chain-smoker of some vile French make of cigarette. The rosy hue of his long nose bespoke his fondness of good French wine and the twinkle in his wicked old eyes of his fondness for bad African women. He soon introduced me to his two resident mistresses; one, a most beautiful 17-year-old metisse (mixed race) called Danielle, and the other, his pride and joy, La Belle Marguerite.

La Belle Marguerite, despite the name, was neither beautiful nor human. She was, in fact, an ugly, ancient, rusting, mildewed flintlock musket that stood against the wall in a corner of his living room. He was enormously proud of it and talked to it as though it were, indeed, human. He even had rows with it when he was in his cups. He sometimes even used it, he said, when he was hunting larger antelopes such as bushbuck and situtunga. The barrel was about five feet long and the weapon operated on black powder. I had seen them in use in my early days in Nigeria and I considered them to be terrifying things.

His cabin was large and wooden. He invited me to stay in his spare room. I accepted his invitation, and soon regretted it. Phillipe and Danielle were both extremely volatile and their nightly disagreements were heroic ones.

Each evening the peace would be shattered by their incessant squabbling over some quite trivial matter. The girl would storm off to bed in high dudgeon, and Phillipe would continue the argument with La Belle Marguerite. When eventually he wandered off to the bedroom, the noise didn't stop there. Phillipe was a lusty old boy and Danielle firmly believed in the old maxim of never going to sleep in anger. Their bed was obviously as old as La Belle Marguerite and the bedsprings badly needed oiling. The wooden floorboards groaned fortissimo in accompaniment to all the racket. Nights, like the days, were bedlam and sleep was well-nigh impossible for me. Eventually, I did the sensible thing and moved out under canvas with my crew.

I had, on this occasion, brought with me a rifle, a Mannlicher .375 express. This had practically been forced upon me by an old white hunter friend in Abidjan before my departure north. The Guiglo area, he warned me, had a lot of bushcow in it and, to those having to live in the forest, bushcow were very bad news indeed. They were a sub-species of buffalo, not much bigger than a Jersey cow, but of fearsome reputation. They were covered in red hair and their temper as uncertain as it was vitriolic.

The African hunters feared bushcow much more than they feared the big black plains buffalo. I had a responsibility for the safety of my crew so – somewhat reluctantly – I accepted his rifle.

It was to prove lucky that I did so, for it was to save my life.

Phillipe called at my camp one evening. A herd of bushcow had taken to visiting the lake to drink, he said, and the old bull in charge had become so cantankerous that the females had driven him away from the herd. Locals called him 'le diable rouge' (the red devil) and he had taken to attacking women and children as they went down to the lake with their buckets to draw water each day. They had begged the Frenchman to kill it for them, as they feared that it would only be a matter of time before it killed someone. He intended to go out the following day with La Belle Marguerite to wait for it, and he would like me to bring my rifle along as back-up.

To say that I was unenthusiastic about the idea would be putting it mildly. But, I felt that I owed him something for his unstinting hospitality when I had stayed at his place, and I certainly had no wish to appear cowardly in the eyes of the villagers.

We hung around the waterhole all day, but while we saw plenty of game, including a small herd of elephant, nary a bushcow did we see. We were on our way homeward in disgust when our guide stopped suddenly, putting his finger to his lips to warn us to be silent. We stayed motionless for what seemed an eternity, straining our eyes at the thickets before us, trying to see what had attracted the guide's attention.

Inevitably, a wayward zephyr betrayed us and our world expoded in a thundering of hooves and a splintering of saplings and our guide vanished with a facility that African guides never fail to exhibit in moments of peril. La Belle Marguerite roared, but it had no more effect upon the Red Devil than a fly swatter would have had. I had a glimpse of mad red eyes and mud-caked, matted hair, then the brute was upon us. It hurled

Phillipe straight up in the air with its short horns and bony forehead, while a glancing blow from one of its flying legs sent me tumbling head over heels into the underbrush. It passed by us in a rushing of wind, spun round, and came back for us again like a locomotive. Fortunately, I had managed to hold on to my rifle. The brute was right on us now. I scrambled frantically up onto one knee and triggered a desperate shot off upward at the enraged beast. More by good luck than by any excellence of snapshooting on my part, the heavy shell went through the animal's throat and shattered its spine. It turned a somersault instantly and landed with an earth-shuddering wallop on its back on the ground between the Frenchman and myself.

I tried to stand, but my knees had suddenly turned to jelly. I sat down hurriedly. The Frenchman crawled on all fours to the body of the bushcow, sat up with his back against it, and lit one of his foul cigarettes. Dust arose in a cloud around the body, little motes of dust that gleamed silver and gold in the African sun.

Phillipe spoke.

'It looks a bit old and tough to be of much use as food for us,' he said critically, 'but no doubt the villagers will have a party with it tonight. I'm sure they'll invite us.'

'Phillipe,' I replied firmly, 'I have lost my taste for bushcow. Tonight, we'll get Danielle to pluck a chicken, and we'll have a small party Chez Phillipe. Just me and you and Danielle.'

'Good idea!' he said. 'And I think we should formally retire La Belle Marguerite at the party. She's showing her years now, don't you think?'

'Yes, Phillipe,' I replied. 'And so am I. I am telling you here and now that I have retired completely from hunting bushcow. And so should you, if you have any sense. If villagers want dangerous animals killed, let them bloody well do it themselves.'

'I'll drink to that!' said the Frenchman.

A few years ago, a friend of mine from my Ivory Coast days told me that Phillipe had died in his sleep at the grand old age of 92 years. His friends had buried him by the verge of Lac St. Jean. La Belle Marguerite was embedded in the concrete tombstone at the head of his grave.

The epitaph reads:

'*Here lies Phillipe, a famous hunter. Beside him, his favourite mistress, La Belle Marguerite. In peace together for eternity.*'

A petrol pump stands today where his cabin used to be, and neither bushcow nor elephant come within fifty miles of the spot.

CHAPTER TWENTY-ONE

The Devil Horse

*'Behold a pale horse, and his name
that sat on him was Death.'*

Revelations 6: 8

To the motion picture aficionado of my childhood, the words 'jungle' and 'monster' and 'spectre' were practically synonymous. Through the Hollywood influence, he was brought up to believe that creatures unknown to civilised man patrolled the dark and mysterious woods of the tropics while the moon was asleep. When, eventually, my travels led me as far as the White Man's Grave, I found the fantasies of Hollywood to be, at times, not all that far removed from reality.

White men would never dream of entering unknown jungles on their own. Black hunters, whose very lifestyle meant that they *had* to enter those wild and uncharted forests, knew exactly what they were doing. They knew by hearsay what horrors those woods *did* contain. They knew all about the monsters and ghouls within, and they knew that only constant obeisance to the appropriate gods would keep them safe from the attentions of those ghastly Things that stalked among the trembling nocturnal shadows.

I am frequently asked by youngsters with over-active imaginations whether I ever saw anything out of the ordinary in my African travels, any sign of any creature I knew to be outwith the bounds of modern zoological knowledge. My answer, sadly, has always had to be in the negative.

'No large and inexplicable footprints around your tent when you went out for a pee in the morning?'

'Certainly not!'

'No great bat-like creatures flying overhead by the light of the silvery moon?'

'Never, thank God!'

'No horrendous, chilling roars echoing out through the still jungle night?'

'Only when the houseboy has forgotten to bring the soda siphon with his master's whisky decanter.'

And off my young inquisitors go, shaking their heads in despair at my deplorable lack of perspicacity in such a promising environment or, more likely, to inform their friends that they have never believed from the beginning that I have ever been nearer the African rainforests than Scotland's Solway Firth.

It pains me to disappoint them. Personally speaking, nothing would please me more than to know that, somewhere out there in those remote forests far from the mechanics of man, there exists some undiscovered relict of the carboniferous era. I too am an incorrigible romantic. Conan Doyle would have found a kindred soul in me. I have no wish to see a real live Tyrannosaurus for myself, mind you, except perhaps from the safety of a heavily armed Royal Navy warship well out to sea, but it would please me mightily to learn that in some dark, forbidding jungle, a disbelieving man of science had come face to face with one such while squatting behind his tent, trousers around his ankles. But if truth be told, I have to record that rarely in all my African travels have I seen anything much more monstrous than myself.

However, there must surely be *something* out there of which we lesser mortals are unaware. Why else would supremely sceptical boffins from reputable institutes of science bother to go out to the swamps of the Congo basin in search of the inexplicable, hoping against hope, each of them, that he or she will be the one to whom fate will accord the honour of finding the next zoological sensation? Hardly a decade passes without reports of yet another collection of eggheads proceeding hotfoot for the Dark Continent complete with the most expensive cameras in the world to record their findings.

In the 1960s there were several such expeditions to my part of Africa in search of 'Mokele-mbembe', a creature said to resemble a plant-eating sauropod of the cretaceous period. The people seeking this creature were by no means cranks – one team was sponsored by the University of Arizona and the other by the Zoological Park of Brazzaville – but each expedition returned home without anything conclusive to report, although many were the pygmy hunters' stories related by them about the legendary beast.

Had they come to me, I could have given them a few more tales to add to their collection. I, too, have been the fascinated recipient of stories from African hunters, including pygmies, on numerous occasions, stories that would have more than held their own at the celebrated 'Liar of the Year Convention' in Okefenoke, Georgia.

For the African hunter is that most obliging of individuals – he will tell you anything to please you. He is also equipped with an inherent shrewdness that belies his country-bumpkin appearance. He can sniff out a cryptozoologist at a range of ten parasangs when the wind is in the right direction. If the learned man is accompanied by a camera crew, so much the better.

Television people are known the world over to be supremely generous. Their pockets are full of other people's money, and they cannot give it away fast enough. The hunter knows that if he plays his cards right and spins a good tale, the rewards will be great. Gone for ever will be all those mosquito-ridden nights of dining on pieces of hairy baboon and maggoty catfish. Tell these asses what they want to hear and the idyllic white man's world of antipodean soap operas and Kentucky Fried Chicken will be his for ever and ever.

I sat with one of these hunters out there in the middle of nowhere once upon a time. We were in a forest clearing in eastern Cameroon; and Shango, the god of thunder, was rumbling in the far distance. It was a night for spirits to be about, if you believed in such things, and although I have always pretended not to do so, the large fire we had sparking and crackling before us was undeniably comforting.

Our conversation drifted round, perhaps inevitably, to a discussion on creatures of the night. 'Moku', he informed me, lived in a huge swamp at the foot of the Kontabili Hills, two days trek to the east, and he came out of the swamp each night to terrorise the local pygmy communities. He had seen it on a number of occasions by the light of his head-lamp while out hunting.

'What is Moku?' I enquired

'Na some kinda terrible animal,' he replied vaguely.

That was as far as his descriptive capabilities would allow him to go. I began to prompt him.

'What colour is it?'

'What colour would you like it to be?'

'How big is it?'

'As big as today and tomorrow.'

'Does it have horns?'

'Yes, three.'

'How long are they?'

'As long as a woman's tongue.'

'Does it have legs?'

'Yes.'

'How many?'

'Four on each side, and one hanging from its throat.'

'A leg hanging from its throat?'

'Yes. I saw it scratching its ear with it, and it was making very terrible noises as it did so.'

I was getting nowhere fast. I threw another stick on the fire and watched the sparks showering upward into the night sky. The little man had fallen silent, lost in a world of his own. A thought came to me. I went to my tent and pulled an old *National Geographic* magazine from my bag. I thumbed through the pages until I found what I wanted. I went back to the fire.

'Is this it?' I asked my black friend.

He peered at the page. His face lit up in recognition and delight.

'Ah! Na he, massa!' he exclaimed excitedly, stabbing his finger at the picture. 'It is Moku! Ah! De very animal! I see 'am plenty times in de Kontabli bush!'

The picture in the magazine was that of a walrus basking contentedly on an Arctic ice floe.

Monsters *do* exist in the swamps of tropical Africa. Of that, I need no convincing at all. But I am equally sure that most of them are simply gross versions of known species; freaks of nature which, such is the inaccessibility of their habitat and the abundance of food within it, have been left in peace to grow to unusual sizes. I am sure of the existence of such monsters because, from time to time, I have encountered them.

The person who, like this author, has had to spend his working life in a tropical rainforest environment, will find that a disproportionate amount of that time is spent in swamp, wading from A to B, and this swamp can be anything from a narrow strip of fairly innocuous marsh to a vastness of putrefaction often reaching up to the armpits. When you find yourself in the latter, it is never easy wading: tree roots are everywhere, unseen by you at the bottom of this great natural sewer of slurry, an endless network of slimy rhizomes over and against which your tortured feet are constantly sliding and slithering and stumbling.

Often at the height of the dry season, these swamp waters stagnate. No water flows into them and no water flows out of them. The swamp dies. To survive in such conditions, a fish must possess one advantage over other fishes - it must be able to breathe air. The clarid catfishes are well adapted to lie in such putrid waters. They have an expanded, lung-like cavity in front of the gills and extending along each side of the spine as a multi-branched structure that is well supplied with blood vessels. As a result, they can breathe air, and this allows them to survive for long periods out of water, provided that their bodies can stay moist enough to keep their thick coating of protective mucus in a constantly slimy condition.

Clarid catfishes are all over Africa, and the biggest member of this family I have ever seen gloried in the scientific name of '*Heterobranchus longfilis*'. Heterobranchus well deserves such a splendid name, for it is one of the more spectacular catfishes, being long and streamlined and of quite beautiful coloration: a delicate pale grey above and milky white below.

The first I ever saw had just been hauled out of an elaborate rattan trap by an old fisherman and it lay grunting horribly on the ground before us until put out of its misery by the old man's machete. Although I had no tape measure with me, I estimated it to be about seven feet long.

Even larger was the first lungfish I ever saw. This curious fish is even more superbly adapted to life in foul water than the clarid catfishes. It breathes almost wholly with its 'lung', to the extent that if it is forced to stay underwater for too long, it will drown. My first encounter with one was when I was driving along a logging track in the Ondo region of Nigeria at the height of the rains, not long after I arrived on my first tour in Africa. I turned a corner on the road and braked sharply. There in front of me was what appeared to be a colossal fish walking up the road in the pouring rain, bolt upright on two skinny but very human-looking legs.

I was stricken with fright. As I write this, half a century after it happened, I feel embarrassed to confess this. My only excuse is that I was still a greenhorn in Africa. In my childhood I had been an avid reader of all the usual Boy's-Own-Adventure type of rubbish about the Dark Continent, without ever quite believing the more lurid of the stories even in those inchoate years when gullibility and I walked hand-in-hand.

Now, all those tales of voodoo rituals and the Walking Dead came vividly to life for me as I watched this astonishing apparition plodding slowly and steadfastly up the muddy road before me in the pouring rain. There was a nameless fear within me, and the clammy sweat that suffused me had nothing to do with the intense humidity of the day. It would have taken very little for me to have turned my vehicle right round and gone back the way I had come. But my home was ahead of me while the way back would simply have led me deeper and deeper into wet and sinister forests; the last thing I wanted, for at that very moment where I wanted to be was to be at home and within easy reach of the whisky bottle.

The downpour and the splatters of mud on my windscreen had made it very difficult to see ahead, and such was the intensity of the rain that sticking my head out of the side window was of no help at all. I think that it was because of the poor visibility that I was suddenly struck with the fervent hope that things, in reality, might not have been quite as spooky as they appeared on the surface. This thought gave me courage to slip the Land Rover into gear and ease it cautiously up the road towards the figure. As I got close to it, I discovered that there was no witchcraft about it; it was, in fact, a villager staggering up the road with an enormous lungfish strapped to his back in such a way that its head and body obscured his own head and body from view, leaving only his legs visible to me on either side of the tail section which trailed on the ground behind him. He gratefully accepted an offer of a lift to his village. Before we humped the ugly, slime-covered brute into the back of my Land Rover, I measured it with my tape measure. It was eight feet and three inches long, well in excess of recorded lengths for this species.

Men of science, God bless 'em, constantly assure us that these are harmless, gentle creatures, no matter their size. The bush African will tell you a different story, and many are their tales of little children vanishing down the gobs of large specimens of these fish. I myself have come upon fishermen with limbs missing; missing, they claimed, as a result of encounters with infuriated lungfish. I doff my hat, as always, to the superior knowledge of these men of science, but I have nevertheless to state that nothing would induce me to wade through an African swamp at dead of night where catfish and lungfish were known to be active. Unless, of course, one of the afore-mentioned boffins was prepared to lead the way.

҂ ҂ ҂

I was in a different part of the White Man's Grave and consider-ably older when I became involved in what Arthur Conan Doyle, that master craftsman of the Sherlock Holmes stories, might have entitled *The Case of the Laughing Horse*. It was a 'case' that puzzled one or two eminent people at the time, and although its resolution owed nothing to my brief and purely chance involve-ment in the affair, and it all happened a long time ago, there are nights even now when the awful, leering visage of that dreadful 'Devil Horse', as it was called by the local hunters, steals silently into my little bedroom to haunt my dreams.

It was in a small mud-walled bar in Zorzor that I first heard of the Devil Horse. Zorzor was in northern Liberia, and it was a very ordinary, dusty little town hugging the border with Guinea. It was a town that, but for the fact that its popula-tion was almost entirely black, could easily have doubled as a Mexican border town in any of Hollywood's less acclaimed Western epics.

My drinking companion on this day was the Area Commissioner, a huge and jovial Liberian.

'You are going to count trees in the Belle Yella forest,' he said.

It was a statement, not a question, for he had already been apprised of the reason for my being here. I replied with a dutiful affirmative and he continued, looking at me seriously as he spoke:

'Be very careful when you are in that bush. There is something bad in there, and you are my responsibility while

199

you are in the area.'

I nodded, remembering what I had heard about the Government's infamous Belle Yella 'Corrective Institute' deep within the forest. It was a prison used mainly for the detention of political misfits, people who had from time to time aired their opposition to the Government's policies in much too strident and public a fashion. Those who entered the prison were never seen again, rumour had it, the reason being that against the event that there might be among them adventurous souls who entertained foolish notions of escape, all new arrivals were actively discouraged from doing so by having their feet smashed with sledgehammers immediately after they had been issued with their prison uniforms.

'Don't worry,' I assured him. 'Nothing would induce me to go anywhere near your Belle Yella prison.'

He gave a thin, dry smile.

'I'm not talking about the prison,' he said. 'I'm talking about the Devil Horse of Belle Yella.'

'Devil Horse?' I gazed at him in disbelief. Ghost stories were ten-a-penny throughout the African bush and I immediately assumed this to be yet another one, a local version of an old and familiar theme. Somehow, though, I had expected something better of him; he was still quite young, despite his high rank, but he had, after all, been educated in the United States of America and had spent a considerable number of years there.

I could not believe that, after all these travels, he still subscribed to this primitive rubbish, this belief in the supernatural so entrenched in the minds of the ordinary hunters and subsistence farmers who had never been any further than the fringes of the great forests around us.

He signalled to the bar, and a girl came over to us with

another two bottles of beer. He refilled his glass and sipped at it pensively, avoiding my eyes. He spoke self-consciously, defensively: 'I'm not saying I believe in it myself, you understand. I'm a good Christian, and good Christians don't believe in ghosts. All the same, there's something not quite right out there…'

His voice trailed off into silence and he fiddled nervously with his tumbler.

'So plenty of people have seen it then? I mean, trustworthy people?'

'Oh yes. Quite a few people have seen it. Not all of them known to me personally of course, but the descriptions never vary in the important aspects. It has been described as having the shape of a large horse, with a rough, pale coat that glows a sort of yellow in the moonlight, a black horse's head with a dark mane, a large shiny white eye, and one very long horn.'

'Like a unicorn, you mean?'

'Well… sort of… except that the horn doesn't stick out of the centre of the forehead, but from the side of its head. Also, it smiles all the time, and it snorts like a horse when it is about to attack.'

'Smiles…?'

I was foundering rapidly.

'Yes, it is a smiling ghost. And oh yes, you may very well laugh. I did too at one time. I didn't believe the stories in the beginning, but I'm not laughing now, and I'll tell you why. The rumours about some frightful creature roaming the forest by night began a couple of years ago. I did not, then, pay a lot of attention to them, putting the stories down to hyperactive imagination fuelled by over-indulgence in our local brand of cane-juice while the hunters concerned were out in the bush at night. Then last year I had to take the stories much more seriously when a couple of my cousins went off on a hunting expedition. They were well into the woods when it suddenly materialized before them. They were too shocked to lift their guns and by the light of the moon they could see that it was smiling a horrible smile at them. It just stood there, smiling at them. One of my cousins lifted his gun and it immediately charged, snorting like a horse as it did so. It hit him amidships and killed him instantly. My other cousin fled for his life. He reported to me that very night and the next day I went with him into the forest with a couple of policemen and some trackers. We recovered the body, and he appeared to have been gored by a single horn thrust. Of the Devil Horse, there was no sign.'

'Didn't you see any prints?'

'None that we could find, but then the ground hereabouts is very hard, consisting almost entirely of raw iron ore. But to tell the truth, none us were of a mind to hang around that place for too long. Can you blame us?' he asked somewhat shamefacedly.

ⵣ ⵣ ⵣ

We sat drinking silently for a time. I was wondering morosely what on earth I was doing sitting here listening to all this nonsense. The day was becoming hotter and hotter by the minute and the clouds of flies defecating around the rim of my glass were enjoying my beer more than I was. I was irritable. Finally, I exclaimed in exasperation: 'It's damn well impossible, man, and well you know it! There's nothing in the whole bloody world looks like what you have described, for Christ's sake!'

He shrugged.

'I said I didn't believe in ghosts myself, and I'm not trying to put you off from going in there. But there's something unpleasant in those woods, that's for sure. As I have said, my poor cousin lost his life through it, and quite a few others since then have had the fright of their lives from it. And, if you make allowances for the usual exaggerations, all the descriptions are so remarkably similar as to make flights of fancy too much of a coincidence.'

'Has this thing ever been seen by day, or only by drunken hunters at night?' I queried caustically.

'My cousin is a Baptist preacher,' he replied coldly. 'He neither drinks nor tells lies. God knows what he saw that night, but you can rest assured that it was as he described it.'

It was not in my best interest to ruffle the feathers of such an august personality as he, and I did my best to placate him.

'I am very sorry; I do not doubt you in the slightest. It is just that it is such an incredible story. But I have work to do in the forest, and I need your help in employing a dozen or so trace-cutters to come in with me.'

'The locals will not go into the Belle Yella bush for love nor money,' he informed me. 'The only people you'll find in there will be Guinea families from over the border, catching and smoking fish from the streams for sale in our local market. They are not afraid, because they believe the Guinea people have a juju to protect them from spirits here. If you need workers, you would be well advised to hire Guinea men, for no Liberian will go in with you. There are plenty of Guinea people hanging around town. I believe you have one Ivory Coast man with you already? How will he react when he hears the story of the Devil Horse?'

'Yes, I have an Ivory Coast man,' I answered gravely. 'His name is Lasana, he is a Fulani, and the only ghosts he fears are Muslim ghosts, especially if they are French speaking. One day he hopes to make it to Mecca, but for the moment he is stuck with me in Liberia, which he considers to be the Muslim equivalent of purgatory. He will be in charge of my crew, and I'll get him busy on hiring suitable workers tomorrow.'

He stood up to leave.

'If your man is a Fulani, he should get on well with the Guinea people,' he said, 'for they, being Mandingo, are just Fulanis by another name. He will have no problem in getting lodgings for as long as you need to stay in Zorzor. But what about you? There is a distinct shortage of 5-star hotels in this part of the world, you know.'

Without waiting for a reply, he continued: 'I have a spare room at home, and I'm sure that my wife would be happy for you to stay with us until you get organised.'

It was an offer I was glad, eventually, to have accepted, for it was to be a full week before Lasana had his crew gathered together and we were ready to enter the domain of the Devil Horse...

At last, though, we were on our way. We were fourteen in number, including Lasana and myself, walking steadily along a little track through the trees, led by Old Sekou, a Guinean fisherman familiar with the area. I had no idea how long we would be away, but I had gone prepared for an initial one-month stay. Old Sekou said he knew of a good camping site in the heart of the forest by the bank of a small stream of good drinking water. The workers were singing happily, a monotonous, hypnotic chant and, without being really conscious of doing so, my step fell in with the rhythm.

I had not known any of the workers before this morning for I had, as always, given Lasana carte blanche in their selection. This meant, of course, that Lasana would inevitably get his cut from each of them out of whatever wages I paid them. It was an old West African custom and much frowned upon by employers who knew nothing of the African way of life, and it is doubtful if the Executive of Britain's Transport and General Workers' Union would have approved. Frankly, it didn't bother me in the slightest; indeed, I rather approved of it, as I did of any system that gave me the minimum of hassle. It was a recognised guarantee of loyalty by the worker to the man who hired him – Lasana – and it was a system that worked well in the Africa of my day. I have never claimed to have any missionary tendencies, and the phrase 'When in Rome…' might well have been coined for me.

I was last in the line, Lasana striding along in front of me, his long, ground-consuming stride taking him effortlessly forward. He has his gun slung over his shoulder, a rather old-fashioned double-barrelled 12-bore shotgun of some cheap Belgian make. I thought about him as we walked. I had known him for some years and he had worked on a number of tree prospections for me. He was a most faithful employee and he was that rarest of West Africans, a devout Muslim who neither drank nor smoked, and whose interest in women was confined to his two wives in faraway Ivory Coast. He was tall and wiry of body, and with an aristocratic mien that gave ample proof of his Fulani forebears. He was a good hunter and bushman, highly intelligent and a tireless worker. His faith in humanity was minimal and he had no faith at all in Liberian humanity.

Being the month of December, it was the height of the dry season and the ground was bone dry. The Belle Yella forest was of outstanding beauty and quite unlike any other forest I had ever encountered in Africa. It consisted almost in its entirety of a strange species called niangon. Niangon is rather small for an African rainforest tree, seldom exceeding 35 metres in height. It has – also unusually for an African rainforest tree – a gracefully sinuous trunk, and it is one that is covered in shaggy bark of a warm autumnal colour that peels off in long, narrow strips to reveal an inner layer of bark of the most delicate shades of pink and lime-green. The leaves are a dark, glossy green on the upper surface and a rich hazel underneath, so that when one looks upward through the canopy while a breeze is stirring the foliage, causing the hazel and the green to shimmer against aquamarine glimpses of the tropic sky, the beauty is quite breath-taking and, in this spectacular forest, it was a beauty enhanced by the clusters of cream and carmine orchids growing in the forks of many of the trees.

We stopped at last at Old Sekou's stream in the heart of the forest. Crystal-clear water trickled through and over the great plates of dark rock that formed the stream bed, aerial ferns and epiphytes of all kinds hung from branchlets swooping low over the water surface from the overhead trees, and enormous lilies grew in riots of purples and yellows in the cool damp patches along the side of the stream.

Leaving the rest of the workers to fix camp, I went with Sekou downstream to where he said his friends from the village were camped. We found them about a couple of miles from where we were establishing our own camp. There must have been about fifty of them, all female, from elderly women to little children. My sudden appearance in their midst startled them more than somewhat at first, but Old Sekou soon put them at their ease.

Their camp was of the crudest kind, consisting of beds laid side by side out in the open under the trees. The beds themselves were simply layers of sticks lashed together with liane and covered with large swamp leaves. Wooden racks covered in little fish being smoked were all around them; small catfish, chiclids, eels, carp, loaches – indeed, just about anything so unfortunate as to find itself in the wicker traps set by the women. Even one large and most unpleasant-looking black cobra that had entered a trap the previous day was now smoking merrily, loop by lethal loop, over the fire before me. A large and mischievous mammy of about the specific gravity of a palm-oil tanker who introduced herself as 'head woman' of the camp offered me a portion of the serpent, the emphatic nature of my refusal arousing much hilarity among the others.

It soon became apparent that a major problem in the Belle Yella forest would be the obtaining of enough food to keep my crew satisfied. The West African man of the forest has always been a highly carnivorous creature, and he needed incredible quantities of meat to keep body and soul together. Without it, he pined, and a pining forest African is a most pathetic sight to behold. Old Sekou could obtain plenty of smoked fish from his contacts among the women of the fishing camp, but, insofar as my crew were concerned, smoked fish was a poor substitute for meat.

The problem here, as in most rainforest areas, was that most creatures were nocturnal. They slept by day and emerged only at night to feed. In Belle Yella the undergrowth tended to be sparse, which meant that the quarry could spot a daytime hunter long before he got anywhere near to being in range. Lasana asked me if I had ever done any night hunting in Liberia. I had, in fact, done so a few times with a Filipino medical friend in the southern part of the country, and I had not very much cared for it. I freely confess that my main objection to it was one that Lasana would not have understood, for the forest African is not in the slightest sentimental about animals. It was just that, to me, there seemed to be something very un-British about creeping up to some poor creature in the dark, then flashing a light into its eyes to dazzle it before blowing it to perdition. However, there was no doubt that, in the African forest, it was a highly effective method of hunting.

'You have a good torch,' he said, 'and we can go out together at night.'

I thought it was a rotten idea, and I demurred somewhat feebly: 'Why don't you take Old Sekou out with you? I will give him the torch.'

Because, he informed me, 'the old man has a girlfriend down at the fishing camp, and his nights are occupied. Anyway, he's too old to come working with us by day and then go hunting with us by night. It will be better with just the two of us. We'll make a good team.'

We certainly did. I held the light for him while he did the shooting, an arrangement that, bloodthirsty though it still was, seemed marginally better to me than doing the shooting myself. We did not kill anything of much consequence – a couple of little duiker antelopes the first night, four guinea fowl on our second night, a couple of large and delicious cane-rats on our third, five more cane-rats on our fourth night – but we kept a well-fed and happy camp as a result.

I gave two cane-rats to Old Sekou to present to his woman at the fishing camp and the gleam in his wicked old eyes when he returned to us the following day told us that the gift had been well-received; too well-received, in fact, for my own comfort, for the old roué informed me that one of the camp women – a damsel called Suki – had fallen head-over-heels in love with me and that, for the modest fee of one cane-rat *per diem*, she would be prepared to share her nights with me.

She was well worth the odd cane-rat, Old Sekou assured me, for she was a lady of considerable sophistication, having learned to cook French food while under contract as exclusive chatelaine to a garrison of Legionnaires in Chad back in the good old days when France had an empire and Maurice Chevalier had begun to thank heaven for little girls.

Somehow, I managed to turn down the proposal without causing offence, and I was relieved to have done so when I met the lady a couple of days later. It was not, I hasten to reassure the more feminist among my readers, that I found her appearance repellent. Quite the contrary. It is possible that Maurice Chevalier might have balked at any suggestion that Suki star opposite him in the musical 'Gigi', but M.Chevalier was no doubt spoiled for choice. I was less so in Belle Yella forest. I found her to have a winsome – if rather snaggle-toothed – smile in a homely black face so wrinkled that it might have been taken by a passing spacecraft on a clear day for a view of the planet Mercury. The merest glance at her mammary glands, however, showed me that in this respect at least, the views of Old Sekou and the great French musical legend might have clashed; having given up the struggle with gravity at about the time of the Kaiser's abdication, they now swung forlornly like empty tobacco sacks in front of her scrawny frame, their southern extremities flirting daintily with her kneecaps as she walked.

But beauty, as the saying goes, is in the eye of the beholder, and Old Sekou obviously found her enchanting. While I would not have gone quite so far as to say that myself, I would have been the first to admit that her smile was cute. What, in the end, put me off was that a career of smoking catfish had impregnated the pores of her skin with a fragrance that would have defied all the wiles of Coco Chanel to eradicate. There is a limit to lust, even for forty-year-old bachelors in the heart of the African rainforests.

☆ ☆ ☆

We had been in the bush for about a month, and our work was near to an end. Lasana and I went out for one last night in the forest, not because we needed any more meat but more so because we had got to enjoy being out in this strange place by night and wanted to experience the pleasure of it one final time. Lasana was carrying his gun, for no other reason than that Lasana would not have left his tent to obey the call of nature at night without having his gun slung over his shoulder.

The heavens glittered with stars. We were making our way along one of the traces we had cleared earlier that day and we were walking in silence, for we had come upon leopard tracks during the day and we did not particularly wish to attract the attention of the creator of them. I had my flashlight in my pocket, but only in case of emergency, for even though there was only a half-moon, there was sufficient light filtering through the loose-leaved crowns of the niangon trees for us to see the way ahead without too much difficulty.

We had walked eight miles or so when a cloud obscured the moon, so we sat down for a breather. We talked in desultory whispers, waiting for the moon to reappear, the whites of Lasana's eyes faintly luminescent in the dim light. A breeze whipped up suddenly, stirring the leaves around us with a dry, rustling sound. Lasana stopped talking, putting his fingers to his lips to warn me to be silent. He turned away from me slowly and with infinite care, onto his knees, indicating that I should do likewise. Crouched on the ground beside him, I strained my ears and thought I could hear the faintest of sounds, as of gravel scrunching under the weight of some large, cautiously moving body. Lasana raised his shotgun, slowly and carefully, two tiny metallic clicking sounds telling me that he was cocking the hammers of his gun.

'Something coming,' he hissed. 'Get ready with light.'

We knelt there, hardly daring to breathe, my heart pumping so loudly that I was sure that whatever was approaching was bound to hear it. Then, seemingly out of nowhere, a large and shapeless silhouette just before us and above us blotted out the starlit heavens and a sudden snorting cough all but ended life's sweet song for me, such was the frisson of shock that surged through my system. Lasana nudged me fiercely in the ribs and I switched on the torch, aiming the beam of light upwards towards the sound. I had a nightmarish vision of a body that glowed a tawny yellow in the light, a hideous black horse-like head crowned by a long, backward-sweeping horn, one lucently-pale eye glaring balefully down at us, and the startling whiteness of large, square teeth exposed in the most hellish of grins, then my night was blown apart in such a blast of sound and flare of light as to both blind and deafen me.

Lasana had emptied both barrels of his shotgun right beside my head so rapidly that both shots sounded as one. A swirling conflagration of light danced crazily around inside my head in a kaleidoscopic firestorm of reds and yellows, but I was aware, even in my dazed state, that Lasana was frantically reloading. I pulled myself together, scrabbled around for the torch, found it, and switched it on. Of the Devil Horse, there was neither sight nor sound. We remained crouching, silent but for our hoarse breathing, our eyes following the beam of the flashlight as I swung it around us, searching the dark woods for any sign of that terrible creature.

I glanced sideways at my companion.

Sweat was running down his face in rivulets and he was trembling as though in an ague.

'It doesn't look like you hit it,' I croaked.

'No sir,' he replied shakily. 'The gun wasn't pointed at it. I got such a fright, I pulled the triggers by accident. I nearly shot your head off instead.'

We sat there for a long time before we felt it safe to move. At last, with a gibbous moon peeking slyly through the roof of the forest, we made our way back to our camp with nothing more ghostly to speed us on our way than the chirrupings of night insects.

𝒳 𝒳 𝒳'

Dr Hiram was an eminent American zoologist, touring wildlife reserves in Africa. We had met briefly during my stint in the Belle Yella area, where he too had been a guest of the Commissioner. Now he was in Monrovia, en route to the USA. I had just encountered him in the bar of his hotel, and I could sense that he was bursting to talk to me. We had not liked each other very much when we had met before, and I could not figure out why he should be so pleased to see me now. He had a reputation for arrogance even in scientific circles, and today he was absolutely full of himself. I was soon to discover why: his was the overweening smugness of a Man of Science about to debunk yet another foolish myth perpetuated with such charming naivety by us incredulous schmucks.

'We found your Devil Horse about a fortnight after you left,' he informed me, 'lying by the side of the road. Stone dead, it was. We think it got knocked down by a truck. The body was fresh, so I had it put in my pickup and taken to Monrovia for an autopsy.'

He toyed with his beer, a satisfied smile playing on his face.

'Your Devil Horse was, in fact, nothing more sinister than a roan antelope.'

'A *roan antelope!*' I exclaimed, staggered.

'Yes,' he said, 'A roan antelope which had had a rough life, but a roan antelope nevertheless. Nothing more devilish than that. It had been badly shot up perhaps a couple of years previously by some hunter with one of those ghastly old dane-guns – you know, the ones they load up with ball-bearings and nails and shit like that. Probably shot at long range, which would explain why it lived on to become a Belle Yella legend, for no vital parts had been hit. But it had received a good spattering of shot along the side of its face, blinding it in one eye and shattering one of its horns. Some of the shot had got it in the muzzle, infecting it so badly that it had eventually begun to decay, exposing its gums and teeth. It must have been able to browse on leaves to a certain extent; at least, enough to keep it alive. But it must have been in constant agony, and this was undoubtedly the reason for its hostile attitude to hunters. It remembered what had caused its pain, and it was taking no chances.'

'But an antelope…?' I interjected in disbelief.

'The roan,' he explained wearily, as though trying to educate a mentally retarded child, 'is, even in normal conditions, a horse-like antelope. It usually lives in savannah, but occasionally it ventures into patches of woodland to browse and to seek shelter from the heat of the day. This one probably wandered in from the savannahs of Guinea after it was shot and, liking the coolness and sanctuary supplied by the forest and the fact that its wounds did not attract flies to the same extent as when it was out in the grasslands, it opted to remain among the trees. Roans are browsers as well as grazers, so it had plenty of food around it, even though it must have experienced difficulty in trying to eat with its wounded muzzle.'

'Poor brute,' I said. 'It was better dead.'

'It was already dying a slow death,' he agreed. 'Its neck wounds had healed a long time ago but its muzzle had been badly shredded and it could never have healed properly. It's just a miracle it lasted as long as it did. Its body was very emaciated. It's a pity your man didn't finish it off the night you both came upon it. I can understand his shock, though. These natives with their primitive superstitions …'

He gave a patronising snigger. 'But I would have expected white people to have more intelligence. Even,' he concluded waspishly, 'British colonials.'

I sat back in my chair, hands behind my head, gazing at him sourly through half-closed eyes, seeing his satisfied little smirk, his horn-rimmed glasses, his Groucho Marx moustache. 'Primitive natives'…. 'Ignorant British colonials'…. Who the hell did this ridiculous little bastard think he was?

I was seething with rage, but I chose my words carefully: 'The only thing Lasana believes in is the Koran. And, unfamiliar as I am with its contents, I should be very surprised if it contains within its pages any reference to Liberia or to its wretched ghosts. Or, for that matter, to smart-ass American scientists who have never been to bush in their lives.'

He favoured me with a wintry smile.

'Perhaps you are right,' he said. 'Bush is for bush people, like you and your black friends. I am an academic.'

Thus it came about, in this most prosaic of ways, that the mystery of the Devil Horse was finally resolved. I never went back to that part of Liberia myself, but I do know that even years after the events I have described, there were many hunters who believed that ghosts of one kind or another still haunted the beautiful forests of Belle Yella. Humanity is like that. Despite all the evidence to the contrary, we choose to believe the impossible, and the more improbable the impossible is, the more we are inclined to believe in it.

Should, however, you happen to be one of those believers and you would like to go to see for yourself, don't let me stop you. Belle Yella will no doubt have changed considerably since my day, but ghosts, I should imagine, will remain the same wherever they are. It is a long and tiring journey from Monrovia to the abode of the Devil Horse, but that should not dissuade a ghost-hunter of your determination. As a gesture of goodwill, I shall even pass on a few survival tips for your holiday out there.

Firstly – and perhaps most important of all – before your departure, withdraw from your bank every cent you possess. You will need it all. Liberian officials have a great love of the stuff, and their fondness for you will increase in direct proportion to the degree of your willingness to grease their palms. Distribute greenbacks as though you have been authorised by a benevolent American government to clear up individual Third World debts once and for all. Start with the distribution on your arrival at Liberia's Robertsfield International Airport, otherwise you will never get clear of the customs sheds.

Once you have the necessary documentation sorted out, it would be greatly to your benefit to spend as little time as possible in Liberia's capital. Apart from its well-merited reputation as the world's wettest capital city, Monrovia is a hellhole of unsurpassed squalidity. It is really no place for a nice person like you. The only entertainment on offer is that which is supplied by garishly-lit Spanish and Turkish dives with names like 'The Rampant Rooster' and 'My Father's Moustache' along the aptly labelled 'Gurley Street'. If you decide to ignore my advice and partake of the delights promised within those establishments, you will, in return, get no more than you deserve. Do not, I strongly urge you, venture from your hotel room at night or you will be instantly and brutally mugged, for Monrovia is host to a greater proportion of villains per capita than any other populated area this side of Tierra del Fuego, not all of them outside the portals of your hotel, either.

The road to Belle Yella runs north from Monrovia. To dignify it with the title 'road' is, however, a joke in the worst possible taste, for it consists of several hundred miles of pot-holed lunacy; a corrugated, jolting, juddering horror more suited to the needs of itinerant cattle drovers than to modern transport. Every forty miles or so you will be required to stop at crude stick barriers which the Liberian Government grandly call 'check-points', manned by evil little toe-rags in battledress, some as young as ten years of age and all as drunk as skunks. Each will be armed with a nasty-looking Israeli or Russian sub-machinegun. It immediately becomes apparent why these barriers are called 'check-points', for this is where those youthful custodians of Liberia's peace and prosperity check you out to see how much money you have in your possession, how many cigarettes you have, whether you are carrying any hard liquor, and whether you are wearing an expensive wrist-watch. From all those items they will be happy to relieve you, to save you the embarrassment of having to hand them over at the next 'check-point' forty miles further on up the road. Give them what they want, for they will certainly shoot you if you don't.

Enjoy your trip. I wish you luck, for you will have much need of it. But I shan't be joining you, no matter what you offer me. I am getting old, and I have grown weary of discomforts associated with adventure. More specifically, I grew weary of Liberia a long time ago.

As for Liberia's ghosts, whether in Belle Yella or elsewhere, I have nothing but sympathy for them. After all, they have to live there.